The Gospel of
MARK

THE MORNINGSTAR VISION BIBLE

by Rick Joyner

MorningStar Publications

The Gospel of Mark, The MorningStar Vision Bible
by Rick Joyner
Copyright © 2013
Trade Size Edition

Distributed by MorningStar Publications, Inc.,
a division of MorningStar Fellowship Church
375 Star Light Drive, Fort Mill, SC 29715
www.MorningStarMinistries.org
1-800-542-0278

International Standard Book Number— 978-1-60708-547-8; 1-60708-547-X

Cover Design: Kevin Lepp and Kandi Evans
Book Layout: Kevin Lepp and Kandi Evans

Unless otherwise indicated, all Scripture quotations are taken from the New American Standard Bible, copyright © 1960, 1962, 1963, 1968, 1971, 1973, 1974, 1977 by The Lockman Foundation. Italics in Scripture are for emphasis only.

For a free catalog of MorningStar Resources,
please call 1-800-542-0278.

The Gospel of Mark
TABLE OF CONTENTS

PREFACE
THE MORNINGSTAR VISION BIBLE
BY RICK JOYNER

Next to His Son and the Holy Spirit, The Bible is God's greatest gift to mankind. What treasure on earth could be compared to one Word from God? There is good reason why The Bible is the bestselling book of all time by such a wide margin. The importance of The Bible cannot be overstated. If Jesus, who is the Word, would take His stand on the written Word when challenged by the devil, how much more must we be established on that Word to take our stand and live our lives by it?

The most basic purpose of **The MorningStar Vision Bible** is accuracy and faithfulness to the intended meaning of the Author, the Holy Spirit. His written Word reveals the path to life, salvation, transformation, deliverance, and healing for every soul who would seek to know God. The universe is upheld by the Word of His power, so there is no stronger foundation that we could ever build our lives on other than His Word. Therefore, we have pursued this project with the utmost care in that what is presented here is His Word and not ours. We were very careful not to let anyone work on it that had an agenda other than a love for the truth and the deepest respect for the fact that we were handling this most precious treasure—God's own Word.

The primary accuracy of any translation is its adherence to the original text in the original languages The Bible was written in, Hebrew and Greek. However, there are problems when you try to translate from a language such as Greek into a language like English because Greek is so much more expressive than English. For example, there are several different Greek words with different meanings that are translated as one word "love" in our English version. The Greek words distinguish between such things as friendship love, erotic attraction, or unconditional love. When we just translate these as "love," it may be generally true, but something basic in what the Author tried to convey is left out. As we mature in Christ by following the Spirit, these deeper, more specific meanings become important. Therefore, we have sought to include the nuances of the Greek language in this version.

A basic biblical guide we used for this work was Psalm 12:6: **"The words of the LORD are pure words; as silver tried in a furnace on the earth, refined seven times."** Every Book we release of this version has been through a meticulous process at least seven times to ensure faithfulness to the original intent. Even so, we do not yet consider this to be a completed work. We are releasing these Book by Book in softcover to seek even further examination by those who read them. We are asking our readers to send us challenges for any word, phrase, or part that you think may not be accurate, along with your reasons. These will be received, considered, and researched with openness. If you have insights that you think should be added to the commentary, we will consider those as well.

You can email these or any comments that you have to bible@morningstarministries.org, or mail them to us at:

MorningStar Publications
375 Star Light Drive
Fort Mill, South Carolina 29715

Please include any credentials that you might have that would be relevant, but they are not necessary for this.

My personal credentials for compiling and editing such a work are first my love for The Bible and my respect for its integrity. I have been a Christian for more than forty years, and I have read The Bible through from cover to cover at least once a year. I do have an earned doctorate in theology from a good, accredited school, but have not used the title because I want my message received on the merits of its content, not by a title. Though I have been in pursuit of knowing the Lord and His Word for more than forty years, I still feel more comfortable thinking of myself as a student rather than an expert. If that bothers you I understand, but when handling the greatest truth the world has ever known, I feel we must be as humble and transparent as possible.

Most of those who have worked on this project with me have been students at MorningStar University. This is a unique school that has had students from ages sixteen to over eighty. Some have been remarkably skilled in languages, especially Hebrew and Greek. Some have been believers and students of the Word for a long time. Others were fairly new to the faith, but were strong and devoted to seeking and knowing the truth. These were the ones that I was especially interested in recruiting for this project because of the Lord's statement in Matthew 11:25:

> **At that time Jesus answered and said, "I praise You, O Father, Lord of heaven and earth, that You did hide these things from the wise and intelligent and did reveal them to babes."**

Because **"God resists the proud, but gives grace to the humble" (see James 4:6; I Peter 5:5 NKJV),** the humility of a relatively young believer can be more important for discerning truth than great knowledge and experience if these have caused us to become proud.

Also, as Peter stated concerning Paul's writings in II Peter 3:15-16:

> **Paul, according to the wisdom given him, wrote to you,**
>
> **as also in all his letters, speaking in them of these things, in which are some things hard to understand, which the untaught and unstable distort, as they do also the rest of the Scriptures, to their own destruction.**

So the untaught can be prone to distort the truth if they are also unstable. This is why the relatively young believers that I sought to be a part of our team were not just stable but strong in the Lord and their resolve to know the truth.

Even so, not everyone who has great knowledge and experience has become so proud that it causes God to resist them. Those who have matured and yet remained humble and teachable may be some of the greatest treasures we have in the body of Christ. Such elders are certainly worthy of great honor and should be listened to and heeded. Nowhere in Scripture are we exhorted to honor the youth, but over and over we are commanded to honor the elders.

So it seems we have a paradox—the Lord reveals His ways to babes, but elders are the ones responsible for keeping His people on the path of life, walking in His ways. This is not a contradiction. As with many of the paradoxes in Scripture, the tension between the extremes is intended to help keep us on the path of life by giving us boundaries. Pride in our experience and knowledge can cause us to stray from this path, as can our lack of knowledge if it is combined with instability. The vision and exuberance of youth are needed to keep the fire of passion for the Lord and His ways burning. This is why the Lord said that the wise brought forth from their treasures things both new and old (see Matthew 13:52).

For this reason, I sought the young in the faith who are also stable and displayed a discipline and devotion to obedience to the truth. I also sought the contributions of the experienced and learned who continued to have the humility to whom God gives His grace. As far as Greek and Hebrew scholars, I was more interested in those who are technically-minded, devoted to details, and who seemed to be free of doctrinal prejudices.

This is not to give the impression that all who worked on this project went over the entire Bible. I did have some who went over the entire New Testament, but most only worked on a single Book, and sometimes just a single issue. I may not have told many of the Greek and Hebrew experts that it was for this project when I inquired about a matter with them.

I realize that this is a unique way to develop a Bible version, but as we are told in I Corinthians 13:12 we "see in part" and **"know in part."** Therefore, we all need to put what we have together with what others have if we are going to have a complete picture. This version is the result of many years of labor by many people. Having been a publisher for many years, I know every editor or proofreader will tend to catch different things, and so it has been with this project. We also realize that as hard as we have worked on being as accurate as possible, we may have missed some things, and we will be genuinely appreciative of every one that is caught by our readers. Again, our goal is to have the most accurate English version of The Bible possible.

Even though accuracy and faithfulness to the original intent of the Holy Spirit were our most basic devotions, we also sought insights that could come from many other factors, such as the culture of the times in which the different Books of The Bible were written. Along with myself, many other contributors have spent countless hours of research examining words, phrases, the authors of the Books of The Bible, their times, and even the history of cities and places mentioned in it. Though the knowledge gained by this research did not affect the words in the text of The Bible, they sometimes gave a greater illumination and depth to their meaning that was profound. Sometimes they made obscure, hard to comprehend phrases come to life.

One of the obvious intents of the Author was to be able to communicate to any seeker of truth on the level they are on. For the most basic seeker, knowing such things as the nuances or more detailed meaning of the Greek or Hebrew words may not be important. As we mature, we will seek deeper understanding if we follow the Holy Spirit. We are told in I Corinthians 2:10, **"For to us God revealed them through the Spirit; for the Spirit searches all things, even the depths of God."** Therefore, those who follow the Spirit will not be shallow in their understanding of anything and will especially search to know the depths of the nature of God.

Our single greatest hope is that **The MorningStar Vision Bible** will accurately reveal the will and intent of the Lord and compel all who read it to love Him more, which is the chief purpose of man. If we love Him more, we will then begin to love one another more. As we grow in love, we will also grow in our devotion to know Him even more, know His ways, and do the things that please Him. He deserves this from us more than could ever be expressed.

There is nothing greater than knowing Him. I am convinced that anything we learn about God will make us love Him more, which is our chief purpose and the one thing that will determine if we are successful human beings. This is also the only thing that can lead to the true peace and true joy that is beyond anything this world can supply. There is no greater adventure that can be had in this life than the true Christian life. The Bible is the map to the greatest quest and the greatest adventure that we could ever experience.

INTRODUCTION
THE GOSPEL OF MARK

The Gospel of Mark found immediate acceptance among the early Christians. There has never been much controversy about its authenticity. It is indeed the work of Mark, who had been a disciple and close associate of several of the most imminent apostles, including Paul and Barnabas.

Mark wrote this account of the life of Christ as it had been told to him by Peter, one of the closest of the twelve to Jesus. Many believe this is why it was written in such a basic and rough style—the way a fisherman like Peter might have conveyed the greatest story ever told. Even though this is the shortest of the Gospels, it includes rich details, such as the expressions, feelings, and gestures of Christ and others in the account, and even comments from the crowd. This implies that the Gospel of Mark is the remembrance of someone very close to Jesus and all that is described. When Mark's Gospel is read with this in mind, its coarse style takes on a special richness.

It is noteworthy that this Gospel is most candid in highlighting the flaws and mistakes of the twelve, especially Peter's. The Bible is unique among religious writings for its transparency about the failures and flaws of even its greatest leaders and heroes. The Gospel of Mark stands out among the other Gospels for this transparency, and as stated, especially concerning Peter. This indicates that even near the end of his life when he was conveying this account to Mark, Peter remained humble and candid about his mistakes. That is the mark of a truly great person.

Unlike the other Gospels, this one starts abruptly with the ministry of John the Baptist declaring Jesus to be the Son of God. Then it describes John as the prophesied messenger sent to prepare the way for the Lord and the beginning of the New Covenant.

Peter had received one of the greatest commendations in the New Testament for first declaring Jesus to be the Messiah and the Son of God from a revelation he had received from the Father. For this reason, Peter was awarded the keys to the kingdom. The ultimate key to the kingdom is the revelation of who Jesus is. Peter uses these keys to open his account of the greatest story ever told—the ministry of Jesus.

The date in which this was written is believed to have been between A.D. 66 and 70, when Mark spent a lot of time with Peter before his execution. This was also just before the destruction of Jerusalem.

NOTES

THE GOSPEL OF
MARK
Mark 1

John the Baptist

1 The beginning of the gospel of Jesus Christ, the Son of God.

2 Even as it is written in Isaiah the prophet, **"Behold, I send My messenger before Your face, who will prepare the way before You"** (see Malachi 3:1).

3 "The voice of one crying in the wilderness, 'Prepare the way for the Lord. Make His paths straight'" (see Isaiah 40:3).

4 John came and baptized in the wilderness, and preached the baptism of repentance for the remission of sins.

5 All of Judea went out to him, and all those who were in Jerusalem, and they were baptized by him in the river Jordan, confessing their sins.

6 John was clothed with camel's hair, and had a leather girdle about his loins, and ate locusts and wild honey.

7 He preached, saying, "There comes One after me who is mightier than I, and the latchet of whose shoes I am not worthy to stoop down and unloose.

8 "I baptized you in water, but He will baptize you in the Holy Spirit."

Jesus is Baptized

9 It was during this time that Jesus came from Nazareth of Galilee, and was baptized by John in the Jordan.

10 Immediately after He came up out of the water, He saw the heavens opened, and the Spirit as a dove descending upon Him.

11 Then a voice came out of the heavens, saying: "You are My beloved Son, in You I am well pleased."

The Wilderness

12 Then the Spirit led Him into the wilderness.

13 so He was in the wilderness for forty days being tempted by Satan. He was with the wild beasts, and the angels ministered to Him.

Calling the Apostles

14 Now after John was imprisoned, Jesus came into Galilee, preaching the gospel of God,

15 saying, "The time is fulfilled, and the kingdom of God is at hand. Repent, and believe in the gospel."

16 Passing along by the sea of Galilee, He saw Simon, and Andrew the brother of Simon, casting a net into the sea, for they were fishermen.

17 Jesus then said to them, "Come with Me, and I will make you fishers of men."

18 Immediately they left their nets, and followed Him.

19 Going on a little further, He saw James the son of Zebedee, and John his brother, who also were in the boat mending nets.

20 He called them, and they left their father Zebedee in the boat with the hired servants, and followed Him.

21 Then they went into Capernaum, and on the first Sabbath day He entered into the synagogue and began to teach.

22 They were astonished at His teaching because He taught them as one having authority, and not as the scribes did.

23 Then a man came into their synagogue with an unclean spirit, and he cried out,

24 saying, "What have we to do with You, Jesus the Nazarene? Have You come to destroy us? I know You. You are, the Holy One of God."

25 So Jesus rebuked him, saying, "Hold your peace, and come out of him,"

26 and the unclean spirit tore him, and crying with a loud voice, came out of him.

27 They were all so amazed that they questioned among themselves, saying, "What is this? A new teaching! With authority He even commands the unclean spirits and they obey Him."

28 So the news of Him immediately went throughout the entire region of the Galilee.

29 When they had come out of the synagogue, they went to the house of Simon and Andrew, along with James and John.

30 Now Simon's mother-in-law lay sick of a fever, and they told Him about her.

31 So He came and took her by the hand, and raised her up, and the fever left her, and she served them.

32 At evening, when the sun had set, they brought to Him all that were sick, and those who were possessed with demons.

33 Everyone in the city gathered together outside of their door,

34 and He healed many that were sick with different diseases, and cast out many demons. But He did not allow the demons to speak, because they knew Him.

35 In the morning, a long time before daybreak, He rose up and went out, and departed into a desert place, and there He prayed.

36 Simon, and they that were with Him, followed after Him,

37 and they found Him, and said to Him, "Everyone is seeking You."

38 So He said to them, "Let us go into the other towns so that I may preach there also. It is for this reason that I came."

39 Therefore He went into their synagogues throughout all Galilee, preaching and casting out demons.

40 Then a leper came to Him, beseeching Him, and kneeling down before Him, saying, "If You will, You can make me clean."

41 Being moved with compassion, He stretched forth His hand, and touched him, and said to him, "It is My will. Be made clean."

42 Immediately the leprosy departed from him, and he was made clean.

43 He sternly charged him before sending him away,

44 saying, "See that you do not say anything to any man about this, but go show yourself to the priest, and offer for your cleansing the things that Moses commanded for a testimony to them."

45 But he went out and began to spread the news about Him everywhere, so much so that Jesus could no longer openly enter into a city, but had to stay in the desert places, and they came out to Him from every place.

John the Baptist

Mark 1:1-8: Mark's style is direct, and he immediately lays out the important facts that establish Jesus as the Messiah.

John was the herald of the Messiah and the New Covenant. However, he did no miracles, and he certainly did not dress for power. He did not start his ministry where everyone else went to seek an audience for their religious message—Jerusalem. Instead, John went to the lowest place on earth, and a difficult place to get to—the Jordan River valley. Yet all of Jerusalem came out to him because he was anointed. Leonard Ravenhill used to say that you do not have to advertise a fire. Those who have the anointing do not have to struggle to preach in certain places to become known. There is no advertising as effective as the anointing.

Jesus is Baptized

1:9-11: John recognized Jesus as the Messiah when the Spirit descended on Him *and remained.* Many are anointed for a time, but upon whom does the Spirit remain? This is the quest of every true disciple—to abide in Him continually and to walk in the anointing to the end.

Having the acclamation of the Baptist was not enough for the Messiah. The Father had to voice His approval of His Son. Jesus was who He was, not by the will of man, but by the will of

God. Many are known by men, but what counts is being known in heaven.

The Wilderness

1:12-13: After such a beginning, one would think Jesus would immediately go up to Jerusalem to be acknowledged. Instead, He does the opposite and goes into the wilderness to be tested by the devil. After such a great acclamation as John gave to Jesus, how many of us would not immediately try to use it to promote our ministry? If we did what Jesus did, going away alone to seek the Father and even humbling ourselves to accept the testing that will inevitably come our way, maybe we could be used in even greater ways and would not be so prone to eventually fall under the weight of our pride.

Calling the Apostles

1:14-45: Jesus preached repentance because the kingdom was at hand, not because judgment was at hand. It was a positive message about what great things were coming, not one that just condemned them because of their behavior. Jesus then demonstrated the power of the kingdom over any condition on earth. That is also how the gospel of the kingdom will be preached at the end of the age.

We also see that at the beginning of His ministry Jesus called the twelve to Himself. The greatest leader of all time did the first thing any successful leader does who would have their impact last after they are gone—He built a team.

NOTES

GOSPEL OF
MARK

Mark 2

Persecuted for Forgiving

1   When He again entered into Capernaum after some days, word was spread that He was in the house.

2   So many were gathered together, and there was no longer room for them, not even near the door, and He taught them.

3   They came, bringing to Him a man sick of the palsy, carried by four men.

4   When they could not come near to Him because of the crowd, they made a hole in the roof over Him, and when they had broken it up, they let down the bed on which the sick man lay.

5   Jesus, seeing their faith, said to the man sick of the palsy, "Son, your sins are forgiven."

6   There were some of the scribes sitting there, and they reasoned in their hearts,

7   "Why does this man say this? He blasphemes! Who can forgive sins but one, even God?"

8   Immediately Jesus, perceiving in His Spirit that they reasoned this way within themselves, said to them, "Why do you reason in this way in your hearts?

9   "Which is easier, to say to this man sick of the palsy, 'Your sins are forgiven'; or to say, 'Arise, and take up your bed, and walk?'

10   "But so that you may know that the Son of Man has authority on earth to forgive sins,'" He said to the Man sick of the palsy,

11 "I say to you, 'Arise, take up your bed, and go to your house.'"

12 So he arose, and immediately took up the bed, and walked out before them all, so that they were all amazed, and glorified God, saying, "We never saw anything like this before."

13 Then He went down by the seaside, and the whole multitude followed after Him, so He taught them.

14 As He passed by, He saw Levi the son of Alphaeus sitting at the place of toll, and He said to him, "Follow Me." He arose and followed Him.

The Friend of Sinners

15 It came to pass that He was sitting down to eat in His house, and many publicans and sinners sat down with Jesus and His disciples, for there were many of these that followed Him.

16 When the scribes of the Pharisees saw that He was eating with the sinners and publicans, they said to His disciples, "Why is it that He eats and drinks with publicans and sinners?"

17 When Jesus heard it, He said to them, "Those who are whole have no need of a physician, but rather those who are sick. I did not come to call the righteous, but sinners."

New Wineskins

18 As John's disciples and the Pharisees were fasting, they came to Him and asked, "Why do John's disciples and the disciples of the Pharisees, fast, but Your disciples do not fast?"

19 Jesus replied to them, "Can the sons of the bridegroom fast while the bridegroom is with them? As long as they have the bridegroom with them, they cannot fast.

20 "However, the days will come when the bridegroom will be taken away from them, and they will fast in that day.

21 "No man sews a piece of new cloth on an old garment, or that which is meant to patch it up will cause an even bigger hole when it shrinks, and worse tear will be made.

22 "No one puts new wine into old wineskins, or the wine will burst the skins, and the wine will be lost along with the skins, so they put new wine into fresh wine-skins."

The Lord of the Sabbath

23 Then it came to pass that He was going through the grain fields on the Sabbath day, and His disciples began to pluck the ears as they went,

24 the Pharisees said to Him, "Look! Why do they do that which is not lawful on the Sabbath day?"

25 Then He said to them, "Did you not read what David did when he had need and was hungry, how he and those who were with him

26 "entered into the house of God when Abiathar was high priest, and ate the showbread that it was not lawful to eat unless you are a priest, and he also gave it to those that were with him?"

27 So He said to them, "The Sabbath was made for man, not man for the Sabbath,

28 "so that the Son of Man is also Lord of the Sabbath."

Persecuted for Forgiving

Mark 2:1-14: Many people think that if legalists could just witness a miracle, they would repent. However, that is not the case, as we see in the New Testament. The greater the miracle that Jesus performed, the greater the persecution that came against Him. The religious ones were more concerned about staying within the bounds of legalistic rigidity than they were for such obvious works of the compassion of God for His people. That is what religion does to the self-righteous.

Everywhere Jesus went, He taught the people, and He healed the sick. The ultimate calling of every Christian is to be like Him and do the deeds He did. As the church becomes the bride of Christ that she is called to be at the end of this age, she will do all the works of Jesus and even greater works as He promised, and she will be like Him.

The Friend of Sinners

2:15-17: Jesus was the most holy Man to ever walk the earth, yet some of the most unholy people were drawn to Him and were comfortable around Him. This will also be the nature of those who are abiding in Him—they will be holy and keep themselves holy, but they will not have the self-righteous spirit that is so repelling to others. Jesus never condoned sin or wayward lifestyles, but sinners could feel His love and respect for them, and they loved Him for it. This is the nature of true religion—it draws the most sinful because they are the ones who know they are in need of God's mercy. These are the ones the Great Physician came to heal.

New Wineskins

2:18-22: People, churches, and even movements can become old wineskins very quickly. A wineskin becomes old when it is too inflexible to receive new wine. This is why in church history there does not seem to be a single group that was used by God for two successive movements. Understanding what makes us become so rigid in our ways, and then learning how to resist becoming rigid, is crucial if we are to continue moving with God.

In this parable, the Lord asserts that He puts new wine into new wineskins in order to preserve the old wineskins too, not wanting them to be lost. New movements should not try to force themselves on the old, but rather respect and honor them, and only go to them when invited. Old wine is actually more valuable than new wine. Even if we are a part of the newest thing God is doing, we must respect the old—the fathers and mothers in the faith—or we will fall from grace very quickly because of our pride. So even if they have become rigid and inflexible, we must honor them and be careful with them, because they too are valuable to the Lord.

The Lord of the Sabbath

2:23-28: Man was not made for the law, but the law was made for man. The Sabbath was not given just to impose something on man, but rather to give man the needed rest and time to seek Him. Beware of legalists who are more devoted to the law than to people for whom the law was made. Law without love is a cruel taskmaster. Love still has rules, but it uses them to set people free, not bind them.

NOTES

THE GOSPEL OF
MARK

Mark 3

Healing on the Sabbath

1   He again entered the synagogue, and there was a man present there who had his hand withered.

2   So they watched Him to see whether He would heal him on the Sabbath day so that they might accuse Him.

3   He said to the man that had his hand withered, "Stand up."

4   Then He said to them, "Is it lawful to do good on the Sabbath day, or to do harm? To save a life, or to kill?" No one answered.

5   When He had looked around at them and beheld their anger, being grieved at the hardening of their hearts, He said to the man, "Stretch out your hand." So he stretched it out, and his hand was restored.

6   Then the Pharisees went out, and along with the Herodians immediately counseled together about how to destroy Him.

7   Jesus withdrew to the sea with His disciples, and a great multitude from Galilee followed, and they also came from Judea,

8   and from Jerusalem, and from Idumaea, and beyond the Jordan, even from Tyre and Sidon, a great multitude, hearing what great things He did, and they came to Him.

9   He told His disciples that a little boat should wait for Him because of the crowd, so that they would not press in upon Him.

10 This was because He had healed many, and there were many who had plagues that pressed upon Him that they might touch Him.

11 Whenever the unclean spirits beheld Him, they fell down before Him, and cried out, saying, "You are the Son of God."

12 He charged them not to make Him known.

Appointing the Twelve

13 He then went up into the mountain, and called to Himself those that He wanted to be close to Him, and they went to Him.

14 There He appointed twelve to be with Him, and that He would send out to preach,

15 and He gave them authority to cast out demons.

16 These were Simon, whom He surnamed Peter;

17 and James the son of Zebedee, and John the brother of James, who He surnamed "Sons of Thunder."

18 Also Andrew, and Philip, and Bartholomew, and Matthew, and Thomas, and James the son of Alphaeus, and Thaddaeus, and Simon the Cananaean,

19 and Judas Iscariot, who betrayed Him.

20 Then He went into a house, but the multitude came together again, so that He could not even eat.

21 When His friends heard it, they went out to lay hold of Him, for they said, "He has lost His mind."

A House Divided

22 The scribes that came down from Jerusalem said, "He has Beelzebub," and, "By the prince of the demons He casts out the demons.

23 And so He called them to Himself, and spoke to them in parables, saying, "How can Satan cast out Satan?

24 "If a kingdom is divided against itself that kingdom cannot stand.

25 "If a house is divided against itself that house will not be able to stand.

26 "So if Satan has risen up against himself, and is divided, he cannot stand, but has come to an end.

27 "But no one can enter into the house of the strong, and spoil his goods, except he first bind the strong man, and then he will spoil his house.

28 "Truly I say to you, all their sins shall be forgiven the sons of men, and even their blasphemies,

29 "but whoever shall blaspheme the Holy Spirit will not be forgiven, but is guilty of an eternal sin."

30 He said this because they said, "He has an unclean spirit."

31 Then His mother and brothers came, and standing outside, they sent to Him, calling Him.

32 A multitude was sitting around Him, and they said to Him, "Behold, Your mother and Your brothers are outside seeking You."

33 And He answered them and said, "Who is My mother and My brethren?"

34 Looking around at those who sat around Him, He said, "Behold, My mother and My brethren!

35 "For whoever will do the will of God, the same is My brother, and sister, and mother."

Healing on the Sabbath

Mark 3:1-12: In this world many people are afflicted with sickness, disease, and physical problems. To have God send His greatest Prophet, His greatest Messenger, His own Son with miracles and healing was a powerful message that He knows their plight, and He wants to help them.

On the other hand, the religious community seemed to have little or no compassion for the condition of the people. They even hardened their hearts more in the face of such extraordinary supernatural works that demonstrated God's love for them. Just to witness God's wonderful works was a great privilege, but they esteemed their own positions and opinions above such miracles and demonstrations of God's compassion

for people. A religious community that is based on legalism esteems precepts and principles more than people—even though those precepts and principles were given to help people.

Appointing the Twelve

3:13-21: You are not a leader if someone isn't following you. The first step to becoming a successful leader is to build a team. The most successful leaders build the best teams. This is what Jesus began to do immediately after He started His ministry.

It is also noteworthy that He called those who might be the most unlikely choices for leadership in a religious movement. Yet this team of seeming misfits became the most effective team in history. A key to having the kind of success Jesus had is to build a team the way He did, beginning with choosing His team the way He did. Jesus did not call those who were already successful, but those He saw potential in. Then He immediately released them to begin doing what they were called to do.

It is also noteworthy that the first thing Jesus called His team to do was draw near to Him. That is the most basic calling of all who would be sent by Him, for we can do nothing except through Him. The closer we abide in Him, the more He can do through us.

A House Divided

3:22-35: The established religious community had a predetermined position that they were the full repository of God's wisdom and purposes. With this mentality, they were bound to reject any new thing that did not come from them. It was also not possible for any new thing to come from those bound by a religious spirit because nothing destroys vision and creativity like this spirit. This caused them to have a predetermined position on anything new—reject it and attack it. Many of their attacks were ridiculous, such as claiming that Jesus cast out demons by the prince of the demons. However, the religiously prideful can seldom see their own foolishness.

After the religious establishment, the next major source of attempted distraction for Jesus and His new movement were His own friends and family. So will it often be with anyone who follows Him today. When the Lord anoints and empowers His servants, they are changed. But those who are closest to them will likely have difficulty relating to them the way they are now instead of the way they once were.

NOTES

The Gospel of
MARK
Mark 4

Parable of the Sower

1 Then a very great multitude gathered to Him as He again started to teach by the seaside. So He got in a boat, and sat a little distance from the shore, with the multitude spread before Him on the land.

2 He taught them many things in parables, saying,

3 "Behold, the sower went forth to sow:

4 "and as he sowed some seed fell by the wayside, and the birds came and devoured it.

5 "Other seed fell on the rocky ground where it did not have enough soil, and immediately it sprang up, but because it had no depth

6 "when the sun arose it was scorched, and because it had no root, it withered away.

7 "Other seed fell among the thorns, and the thorns grew up, and choked it, and it yielded no fruit.

8 "Others fell into the good ground, and yielded fruit, growing up and increasing, some bringing forth, thirty times as much, some sixty, and some one hundred times what was sown."

9 Then He said, "Who has ears to hear, let him hear."

10 When He was alone, they that were close to Him, along with the twelve asked the meaning of the parables.

11 He replied to them, "To you it has been given to understand the mysteries of the kingdom of God, but to them that are without they are spoken to in parables,

12 "so that seeing they may see, and not perceive, and hearing they may hear, and not understand, lest they should repent and be forgiven."

13 He said to them, "Do you not understand this parable? How then will you understand any of the parables?

14 "The seed that was sown is the word.

15 "These are the ones by the wayside where the word is sown. When they have heard the word immediately Satan comes, and takes away that which was sown in them.

16 "The others are like those where the seed is sown upon the rocky places, who, when they have heard the word immediately receive it with joy,

17 "but they have no root in themselves, and endure for just a little while. When tribulation or persecution arises because of the word they quickly stumble.

18 "Others are like the ones where the seed is sown among the thorns.

19 "These receive the word, but the cares of the world, and the deceitfulness of riches, and the lusts for other things enter in, choke the word, and it becomes unfruitful.

20 "Then there are those who are like the seed that is sown upon the good ground. These hear the word, and accept it, and bear fruit, some thirtyfold, some sixtyfold, and some one hundredfold."

Being the Light

21 He then said to them, "Is the lamp brought to be put under a bushel basket, or under a bed, and not to be put on the stand?

22 "For there is nothing hidden except that it should be manifested. Neither was anything made a secret that will not come to light.

23 "If any man has ears to hear, let him hear."

24 He continued, "Take heed to what you hear. With the same measure that you give it out it shall be measured to you, and even more shall be given to you.

25 "For he that has much, to him shall more be given. He that does not have much, even that which he has will be taken away from him."

The Kingdom is Like Seed

26 Then He said, "So the kingdom of God is like a man who casts seed upon the earth;

27 "and though he sleeps at night and rises in the day, the seed sprouts and grows up, but he does not know how.

28 "The earth bears fruit by herself, first the blade, then the ear, then the full grain of the ear.

29 "When the fruit is ripe immediately he puts forth the sickle, because the harvest has come."

30 He said, "To what shall we liken the kingdom of God? Or in what parable shall we explain what it is like?

31 "It is like a grain of mustard seed, which, when it is sown upon the earth, though it is smaller than all the seeds that are upon the earth,

32 "yet when it is sown, it grows up, and becomes greater than all the herbs, and puts out great branches so that the birds of the heavens can lodge under the shadow of it."

33 With many such parables He taught them, and they were able to understand.

34 Yet He did not speak to the people except through parables, but privately He expounded on all of these things to His own disciples.

35 On that day, when evening had come, He said to them, "Let us go over to the other side."

Calming the Storm

36 Leaving the multitude they took Him with them, as He was already in the boat. Other boats also came with Him.

37 Then there arose a great storm with wind, and the waves washed over the boat so that the boat began to fill.

38 He was in the stern, asleep on the cushion. So they awoke Him saying, "Teacher, do You not care that we are about to perish?"

39 So He arose, and rebuked the wind, and said to the sea, "Peace. Be still." The wind immediately ceased, and there was a great calm.

40 He said to them, "Why are you so fearful? Do you not yet have any faith?"

41 But they were terrified, and said one to another, "Who then is this, that even the wind and the sea obey Him?"

Parable of the Sower

4:1-20: We know the Lord desires for all to be saved and come to the knowledge of the truth. Yet here He says that only His disciples will be given the understanding of the kingdom of God, and the multitudes will be spoken to in parables so they will not be able to understand. How can both of these be so?

First, throughout the Lord's teachings He makes clear what it takes to become a disciple, such as doing all things for the sake of the kingdom and being willing to take up the cross daily. In John 7:17 Jesus says:

"If any man is willing to do His will, he shall know of the teaching, whether it is of God, or *whether* I speak from Myself."

Here we see that a prerequisite for understanding His truth is being willing to obey Him.

One of the great questions has been: "Do we need faith to understand, or do we need understanding in order to have faith?" Here the Lord answers that question and makes it clear that we must have faith to be willing to obey before we will be given understanding. His disciples left everything to follow Him, which was an ultimate demonstration of their faith in Him. Therefore, they were given full understanding of everything.

As we are told in the Parable of the Sower, just being given understanding does not mean we will bear fruit. Who honors His word to the degree that they will cultivate it? Cultivation requires preparing the soil for seed, sowing the seed, keeping it watered, keeping out the weeds which are the cares and worries of this world, etc. Do we esteem His word enough to do this? Do we take the understanding we are given from sermons, books, or other sources and cultivate them so that we may bear fruit with them?

If we are honest with ourselves, we should be able to quickly determine what kind of soil we are. How many believers sit under great and anointed teaching for years and love it, but are not really doing anything with it? They are therefore not bearing any fruit.

Being the Light

4:21-25: Our purpose on this earth is not just to have the light, but to share it. Hiding the light we have been given from those who so desperately need it may be one of the greatest crimes we could commit.

The Kingdom is Like Seed

4:26-35: Comparing the kingdom to seed that is sown and grows is a basic revelation of how the kingdom is ever growing and expanding. As Isaiah wrote, there shall be no end to the *increase* of His authority, which is His kingdom. Therefore, if we are living in the kingdom, we will always be growing, spreading, and multiplying. As the Lord taught, there will be times of pruning and cutting back, but this will only last for a season, and then there will be even more fruit. In nature anything that stops growing has started dying. The kingdom will never die, so it will never stop growing. Are we still growing?

Calming the Storm

4:36-41: The Lord upholds the universe with His word. To calm a storm on this tiny little planet was a small thing for Him. Even so, this was the authority He had given to man to rule over the earth. Jesus did not come to show us the power He had in heaven, but what we could walk in here, if we would abide in Him.

NOTES

The Gospel of
MARK
Mark 5

Legion

1 When they came to the other side of the sea, into the country of the Gerasenes.

2 and He had come out of the boat, immediately a man with an unclean spirit came out of the tombs to meet Him.

3 This man dwelt among the tombs, and no one could bind him, not even with a chain.

4 When they had tried to bind him with fetters and chains, he tore them asunder, and broke the fetters into pieces. So no man had the strength to capture him.

5 So continually, night and day, he cried out in the tombs and in the mountains, and would cut himself with stones.

6 When he saw Jesus from a distance, he ran and worshiped Him,

7 crying out with a loud voice, saying, "What do I have to do with You, Jesus? You are the Son of the Most High God. I adjure You by God not to torment me!"

8 For He said to him, "Come out of the man, you unclean spirit."

9 So He asked him, "What is your name?" The demon said to Him, "My name is Legion, for we are many."

10 So he implored Him not to send them out of the country.

11 Now there was on the mountainside a great herd of swine feeding.

12 So they beseeched Him, saying, "Send us into the swine that we may enter into them."

13 He gave them permission, and the unclean spirits came out, and entered into the swine. Then the herd rushed down the steep bank into the sea. There were about two thousand, and they all drowned in the sea.

14 When those who kept the swine went and told about this in the city and throughout the country, many came to see what had happened.

15 When they came to Jesus, and saw the one that had been possessed with demons sitting, clothed, and in his right mind, the very one who had legion, they were afraid.

16 When they considered what had happened to the man who was possessed with demons, and the swine,

17 they began to ask Him to depart from their region.

18 As He was entering into the boat, the one that had been possessed with demons asked if he might come with Him.

19 But He did not permit this, but said to him, "Go to your house, to your friends, and tell them about the great things that the Lord has done for you, and how He had mercy on you."

20 So he went his way, and began to publish in Decapolis how Jesus had done such great things for him, so that all who were in that region marveled.

21 When Jesus had crossed over again in the boat to the other side, a great multitude gathered to Him, as He was by the sea.

22 There also came one of the rulers of the synagogue, Jairus by name, who seeing Him fell at His feet,

23 and beseeched Him greatly, saying, "My little daughter is at the point of death. I pray that You will come and lay Your hands on her so that she may be made whole and live."

24 So He went with him, and a great multitude followed, and they thronged Him.

Touching the Hem of His Garment

25 There was a woman in the crowd who had an issue of blood for twelve years.

26 She had suffered greatly at the hands of many physicians, and had spent all that she had, and was still not healed, but rather grew worse.

27 Having heard the things concerning Jesus, she came through the crowd behind Him, and touched His garment.

28 For she said, "If I but touch His garments, I will be made whole."

29 Immediately the issue of her blood ceased, and she felt it in her body, and knew that she was healed of her plague.

30 Jesus immediately perceived in Himself that power had gone forth from Him, and so turned around in the middle of the crowd, and said, "Who touched My garments?"

31 His disciples said to Him, "Do You not see this multitude thronging You? How do You say, 'Who touched Me?'"

32 Even so, He looked around to see the one that had done this.

33 So the woman, fearing and trembling, knowing what had been done to her, came and fell down before Him, and told Him everything.

34 He said to her, "Daughter, your faith has made you whole. Go in peace and be healed of your affliction."

Resurrecting Jairus' Daughter

35 While He was still speaking, they came from the ruler of the synagogue's house saying, "Your daughter is dead. Why trouble the Teacher any further?"

36 Jesus, not heeding what was spoken, said to the ruler of the synagogue, "Do not fear, but believe."

37 So He did not allow anyone to follow with Him, except Peter, and James, and John the brother of James.

38 They come to the house of the ruler of the synagogue, and He beheld a tumult, as many were weeping and wailing.

39 When He had entered in, He said to them, "Why do you make such a tumult and cry? The child is not dead, but sleeps."

40 Then they laughed at Him, and scorned. After putting them all out, He took the father of the child, and her mother, and those who were with Him, and went in to where the child was laying.

41 Taking the child by the hand, He said to her, "Tabitha, cumi." Which being interpreted is, "Girl, I say to you, 'Arise.'"

42 Immediately the girl rose up, and walked, for she was twelve years old. They were all astonished, and in great amazement.

43 He then charged them solemnly that no man should know this. And He directed them to give her something to eat.

Legion

Mark 5:1-24: In the previous chapter, a great storm had come up as Jesus and His disciples were crossing over the sea. In other Gospels it says that Jesus "rebuked" the storm. This is because some storms are demonic. It is likely that this storm was being stirred up to protect Legion, as this horde seemed to be anticipating Jesus' arrival. The point is that there are demonic storms. Not all storms are, of course, but there are some you can feel the evil presence in, and we can have authority over them in Christ.

We are not told in this narrative how this man came to be possessed with so many demons. However, we are given the principle in the Gospels that if a demon is cast out, it will always seek to return. If it returns and its place has not been filled with that which is God's counter to the evil, then it will not only take its place again, but bring seven more even worse than itself. This is like getting rid of a gopher but not filling in the holes it has made, so more gophers come.

The good thing about this lesson is that as deep as the devil has gotten into someone, to that depth the Lord can fill them. His strength is made perfect in weakness, so whatever had a grip on us can become the basis of a greater good.

Touching the Hem of His Garment

5:25-34: In the other Gospels, this woman touched the hem of His garment to be healed. The high priest in the Old Testament had pomegranates and bells interspersed and sown around the hem of his garment. Pomegranates were

used for medicine, and therefore spoke of healing. Bells spoke of a proclamation. These were prophetic symbols, and every time the high priest moved, the message of healing went forth. That this woman wanted to specifically touch the hem of His garment could mean she recognized Jesus as the true High Priest. Whether this is so or not, Jesus is the true High Priest, and wherever He went, the message of healing did go forth. It still does today.

It is also noteworthy that while Jesus was being thronged by a crowd, this woman touched Him with a faith that released His power. Many people throng Jesus, but there is a difference in pressing in upon Him and touching Him with faith.

Raising Jairus' Daughter

5:35-43: This was the first resurrection Jesus performed. The next person had been dead longer and was about to be buried. The last one, Lazarus, had been in the grave for four days. So each resurrection became more spectacular. With such extraordinary demonstrations of God's power, one would think even the most hardened hearts would have melted. They did not. Rather, they became even more resistant to Him. The persecution against Jesus grew with the increasing power He demonstrated. We are naïve to think that miracles will convince skeptics; miracles are not given for this reason. Miracles are given simply because God loves people and wants to heal them.

NOTES

THE GOSPEL OF
MARK

Mark 6

Rejected by His Own

1 He went out from there, and came into His own country, and His disciples followed Him.

2 When the Sabbath had come, He began to teach in the synagogue, and many after hearing Him were astonished, saying, "Where did this man get these things? What is the wisdom that has been given to this man, *and the power* to do such mighty works that are wrought by His hands?

3 "Is this not the carpenter, the son of Mary, and brother of James, and Joseph, and Judas, and Simon? Are not His sisters here with us?" So they were offended by Him.

4 Jesus then said to them, "A prophet is not without honor except in His own country, with His own kin, or within His own house."

5 Therefore He could not do any miracles there, except to lay His hands upon a few sick people and heal them.

6 He marveled at their unbelief, and went around to the other villages teaching.

The Twelve Sent Out

7 Then He called the twelve to Himself, and began to send them out two by two, and He gave them authority over the unclean spirits.

8 He charged them that they should take nothing for their journey, except for a staff; no bread, no wallet, and no money in their purse,

9   but to go shod only with sandals, and not to put on two coats.

10 He said to them, "When you enter into a house, abide there until you leave that city.

11 "If a place does not receive you, and they will not hear you, as you go forth, shake off the dust that is under your feet for a testimony to them."

12 So they went out, and preached that men should repent.

13 They cast out many demons, and anointed many with oil that were sick, and healed them.

14 Even King Herod heard of it, for His name had become known, and he said, "John the Baptizer has risen from the dead, and therefore these powers now work in Him."

15 But others said, "It is Elijah." Others said, "It is a prophet, even as one of the prophets of old.

John the Baptist Martyred

16 When Herod heard of it, he said, "John, whom I beheaded, he has risen."

17 For Herod himself had sent and arrested John, and bound him in prison for the sake of Herodias, his brother Philip's wife, whom he had married.

18 For John said to Herod, "It is not lawful for you to have your brother's wife."

19 So Herodias set herself against him, and wanted to kill him, but she could not.

20 Because Herod feared John, knowing that he was a righteous and holy man, he kept him safe. When he heard him, he was moved in many ways, and he liked to listen to him.

21 When his birthday came, Herod made a feast for his lords, and the captains, and the chief men of Galilee.

22 When the daughter of Herodias herself came in and danced, she pleased Herod, and those who sat at the dinner with him, and the king said to the girl, "Ask of me whatever you will, and I will give it to you."

23 Then he swore to her, "Whatever you will ask of me, I will give it you, even to the half of my kingdom."

24 So she went out, and said to her mother, "What should I ask for?" She said, "The head of John the Baptist."

25 Then she came in straightway with haste to the king, and asked, saying, "I want you to give me right now on a platter the head of John the Baptist."

26 The king was distraught, but for the sake of his oath, and his guests, he would not reject her.

27 Immediately the king sent a soldier from his guard, and commanded him to bring his head. So he went and beheaded him in the prison,

28 and brought his head on a platter, and gave it to the girl, and the girl gave it to her mother.

29 When his disciples heard of it, they came and took his corpse, and laid it in a tomb.

Feeding the Five Thousand

30 Then the apostles gathered back to Jesus, and they told Him all of the things that they had done, and the things that they had taught.

31 Then He said to them, "Come apart into a desert place, and rest for a while." Because there were many coming and going, and they had no leisure even for taking a meal.

32 So they went away in the boat to a desert place away from the crowds.

33 But the people saw them going, and many knew where they were going, and they ran together to the place on foot from all the cities, and got there before He did.

34 When He saw such a great multitude, He had compassion on them, because they were like sheep without a shepherd, and He began to teach them many things.

35 So when the day was almost gone, His disciples came to Him, and said, "The place is a desert, and the day is now over.

36 "Send them away so that they may go into the country and villages around, and buy themselves something to eat."

37 He answered and said to them, "You give them something to eat." They therefore replied to Him, "Shall we go and buy hundreds of dollars worth of bread and give them food?"

38 He said to them, "Go and see how many loaves you have." When they had found out, they said, "Five, and two fish."

39 Then He commanded them to have all the people sit down in groups upon the grass.

40 So they sat down in groups of hundreds and fifties.

41 Then He took the five loaves and the two fish, and looking up to heaven, He blessed them, and broke the loaves; and He gave it to the disciples to set before the people. The two fish were shared by everyone.

42 They all ate until they were filled.

43 Then they took up the broken pieces of bread that were left over, and there were twelve basketfuls, and a lot of fish.

44 Those who ate the bread were five thousand men.

45 Then immediately He commanded His disciples to enter into the boat, and to go before Him to the other side, to Bethsaida, while He Himself sent the multitude away.

46 After He had taken leave of them, He departed into the mountain to pray.

Walking on Water

47 When evening had come, the boat was in the middle of the sea, and He was alone on the land.

48 As He saw them having difficulty rowing, for the wind was against them, during the fourth watch of the night He came to them, walking on the sea, and He intended to pass by them,

49 but when they saw Him walking on the sea, they thought that it was a ghost, and cried out.

50 For they all saw Him, and were terrified. Then He spoke to them, and said, "Be encouraged: it is I. Do not be afraid."

51 He went up to them and got into the boat, and immediately the wind stopped, and they were all astonished.

52 They had not understood about the loaves, but their hearts were hardened.

53 When they had crossed over, they came to the land of Gennesaret, and moored the boat to the shore.

54 When they got out of the boat, immediately the people recognized Him,

55 and ran round about that whole region, and began to carry on their beds those that were sick, where they heard that He was.

56 Wherever He entered into villages, or into cities, or into the country, they laid the sick in the marketplaces, and sought Him that they might touch even the border of His garment, and as many as touched Him were made whole.

Rejected by His Own

Mark 6:1-6: It would seem that those who knew Jesus best would be the most thrilled by what He was doing, but it was not so. There is a saying that "familiarity breeds contempt." This may be why almost every person who excels or reaches great heights in something must leave their home, familiar surroundings, and closest people to do so. This is why Abraham had to go out from Chaldea. Jacob and Joseph also had to leave their homes to become what they were called to be. Often it is those who know us best, and who may love us most, who will hold us back.

When I was young and The Beatles were climbing in international fame, an article told how their fans at the old club in Liverpool where they started out were distressed by their fame. They actually wanted The Beatles to give up their international success and come back so they could keep what they had going in their little club. Such a mentality may be why Jesus instructed those He sent out not to "greet anyone on the way." In those times, a person only greeted close friends or relatives. These are the very ones who will hold us back from

our destiny, and often must be avoided, if we are going to reach that destiny.

If we prone to get our encouragement or be discouraged by how we are viewed by close friends or relatives, it can keep us from our purpose. The Apostle Paul said that if he were still seeking to please men, he would not be a bondservant of Christ (see Galatians 1:10). If we are going to fulfill our purpose in Christ, we must live our lives for Him above all others.

The Twelve Sent Out

6:7-15: The Lord was quick to release His disciples into ministry. This same account is found in Luke 10. In the next chapter, Luke 11, they came and asked Him to teach them to pray. This means He sent them out to preach the gospel, cast out demons, and heal the sick before they even knew how to pray. How different this is than what we tend to require of people before we release them into ministry. Could this be why there is so much difference in the results as well?

John the Baptist Martyred

6:16-29: John the Baptist was the last of the Old Covenant order of prophets, as well as the first of the New Covenant order. Jesus called him the greatest man ever born of woman. He is also a model for all ministry—to prepare the way for the Lord and point to Him so that all will follow Him, while being willing to decrease as He increased. It was fitting that such a one would be honored with martyrdom.

Feeding the Five Thousand

6:30-46: There is no lack in the kingdom. Whatever the King blesses so that it is touched by heaven will be multiplied on the earth. Whatever the King blesses will be enough for those who follow Him.

Walking on Water

6:47-56: The authority of the kingdom of heaven trumps all natural laws. Natural laws submit to the King, not the other way around. This is why Jesus could walk on water, or could have walked on air if He had so chosen.

When our God walked the earth, He preached the kingdom, He healed, and He set captives free. He was bringing the authority of the kingdom of heaven to earth. He has not changed. This is what He still does when He moves in His people.

NOTES

THE GOSPEL OF
MARK

Mark 7

Worshiping Traditions Instead of God

1   There were Pharisees and scribes who came to Him from Jerusalem.

2   These observed that some of His disciples ate their bread with defiled, or, unwashed hands.

3   The Pharisees, and indeed all of the Jews, will not eat except they wash their hands diligently, holding to this tradition of the elders.

4   When they come from the marketplace, except they bathe themselves they will not eat. There are also many other traditions that they hold to like the washing of cups, pots, and brazen vessels.

5   So the Pharisees and the scribes asked Him, "Why do Your disciples not walk according to the tradition of the elders, but eat their bread with defiled hands?"

6   So He said to them, "Isaiah accurately prophesied of you hypocrites, as it is written, '**This people honor Me with their lips, but their heart is far from Me.**

7   "'**In vain do they worship Me, teaching as their doctrines the precepts of men**' (see Isaiah 29:13).

8   "You overlook the commandments of God, but hold fast the tradition of men.

9   "You reject the commandment of God so that you may keep your tradition.

10 "For Moses said, '**Honor your father and your mother;**' and, '**He that speaks evil of father or mother, let him be put to death.**'

11 "But you say, 'If a man says to his father or his mother, 'That with which you might have been helped by me is 'already given to God.'

12 "You no longer suffer him to do anything for his father or his mother,

13 "and make void the word of God by your tradition that you have conceived. There are many such things as this that you do."

14 He called to Himself the multitude again, and said to them, "Hear Me, all of you, and understand:

15 "There is nothing from without that going into a man can defile him, but the things that proceed out of the man are those that defile the man.

16 "If any man has ears to hear, let him hear."

17 When He had entered into the house away from the multitude, His disciples asked Him about the parable.

18 So He said to them, "Are you without understanding also? Do you not perceive that whatever from without that goes into the man, it cannot defile him;

19 "because it does not go into his heart, but into his belly, and then passes out?" This He said, making all meats clean.

20 He continued saying, "That which proceeds out of the man is what defiles the man.

21 "For from within, from out of the heart of men, come evil thoughts, fornications, thefts, murders, adulteries,

22 "coveting, wickedness, deceit, lasciviousness, an evil eye, railing, pride, and foolishness.

23 "These evil things proceed from within, and defile the man."

Crumbs from His Table

24 Then He arose, and went away to the borders of Tyre and Sidon. There He entered into a house, and did not want anyone to know it, but He could not be hidden.

25 Immediately a woman, whose little daughter had an unclean spirit, having heard of Him, came and fell down at His feet.

26 This woman was a Greek, a Syrophoenician by race. She beseeched Him to cast the demon out of her daughter.

27 He replied to her, "Let the children first be filled, because it is not right to take the children's bread and cast it to the dogs."

28 So she answered and said to Him, "Yes, Lord, but even the dogs under the table eat the children's crumbs."

29 He then said to her, "For this saying, go your way; the demon has gone out of your daughter."

30 So she went away to her house, and found the child laid upon the bed, and the demon had gone out.

31 Then He went out from the borders of Tyre, and came through Sidon to the sea of Galilee, through the borders of Decapolis.

32 There they brought to Him one that was deaf, and had an impediment in his speech, and they asked Him to lay His hand upon him.

33 So He took him aside from the multitude privately, and put his fingers into his ears, and He spat, and touched his tongue.

34 Then, looking up to heaven, He sighed, and said to him, "Ephphatha," that is, "Be opened."

35 His ears were opened, and the bond of his tongue was loosed, and he spoke plainly.

36 Even though He charged them that they should tell no man, but the more He charged them the more they made a great deal of it, and published it abroad.

37 They were astonished beyond measure, saying, "He has done all things well; He makes even the deaf to hear, and the dumb to speak."

Worshiping Traditions Instead of God

Mark 7:1-23: It is an evil, religious spirit that would have us basing our relationship to God on religious performance rather than on our relationship with Him gained for us by the cross of Jesus. This religious spirit will cause people to judge others more severely on their conformance to rituals and traditions

rather than the most important thing of all—loving God and loving one another.

As Mark noted here, when the Lord explained that it was not what went into a person, such as food, that defiled him, He was essentially making all food clean and acceptable. He later verified and established this in His revelation to Peter, which led to the first Gentile converts.

Crumbs from His Table

7:24-37: God resists the proud but gives His grace to the humble. This humility on the part of the Gentile woman could not but provoke the grace of God. Humility combined with faith is a powerful combination in moving the heart of God.

NOTES

THE GOSPEL OF
MARK
Mark 8

Feeding the Multitude

1 In those days there was again a great multitude gathered, and they had nothing to eat, so He called His disciples to Himself and said to them,

2 "I feel compassion for the multitude, because they have continued with Me now for three days, and have nothing to eat.

3 "If I send them away fasting to their home, they will faint on the way, and some of them have come from far away."

4 His disciples answered Him, "With what shall one be able to fill these men with bread here in a desert?"

5 He asked them, "How many loaves do you have?" They said, "Seven."

6 He commanded the multitude to sit down on the ground, and He took the seven loaves, and after giving thanks, He broke them, and gave them to His disciples to set before them, and they set them before the multitude.

7 They also had a few small fishes, and having blessed them, He commanded to set these before them also.

8 So they all ate, and were filled, and they took up the leftover pieces that remained, and there were seven baskets.

9 There were about four thousand, and He sent them away.

10 Immediately He entered into the boat with His disciples, and came into the parts of Dalmanutha.

Seeking a Sign from Heaven

11 The Pharisees came up to Him, and began to question Him, seeking a sign from heaven from Him in order to test Him.

12 He sighed deeply in His Spirit, and said, "Why does this generation seek a sign? Truly I say to you that there shall no sign be given to this generation."

13 So He left them, and again entering into the boat departed to the other side.

14 But the disciples forgot to take bread, and they did not have more than one loaf with them.

15 And He charged them, saying, "Take heed, and beware of the leaven of the Pharisees, and the leaven of Herod."

16 So they reasoned with one another, saying, "We have no bread."

17 Jesus, perceiving this, said to them, "Why do you think that I say this because you have no bread? Do you not yet perceive, neither understand? Is your heart hardened?

18 "Having eyes, do you not see? Having ears, do you not hear? Do you not remember?

19 "When I broke the five loaves to give to the five thousand how many baskets full of broken pieces did you take up?" They answered, "Twelve."

20 "When I broke the seven *loaves* among the four thousand, how many basketfuls of broken pieces did you take up?" They answered Him, "Seven."

21 So He said to them, "Do you not yet understand?"

Healing the Blind Man

22 So they came to Bethsaida where they brought to Him a blind man, and asked Him to touch him.

23 He took hold of the blind man by the hand, and brought him out of the village, and when He had spit on his eyes, and laid His hands upon him, He asked him, "Do you see?"

24 He looked up, and said, "I see men like trees, walking."

25 Then again He laid His hands on his eyes, and he looked steadfastly, and was restored, and saw all things clearly.

26 He sent him away to his home, saying, "Do not even enter into the village."

The Great Confession

27 Jesus went with His disciples into the villages of Caesarea Philippi, and on the way He asked His disciples, "Who do men say that I am?"

28 They answered Him, saying, "Some say John the Baptist, and others say Elijah, but others, one of the prophets."

29 He then asked them, "But who do you say that I am?" Peter answered and said to Him, "You are the Christ."

30 He charged them that they should tell this to no one.

31 Then He began to teach them, saying that the Son of Man must suffer many things, and be rejected by the elders, and the chief priests, and the scribes, and be killed, and after three days rise again.

32 He said this plainly, but Peter took Him aside, and began to rebuke Him.

33 He then turned about, and looking at His disciples, He rebuked Peter, saying, "Get behind Me, Satan! You are not setting your mind on the things of God, but the things of men."

34 Then He called to Himself the multitude, along with His disciples, and said to them, "If any man would follow Me, let him deny himself, and take up his cross, and follow Me.

35 "For whoever would save his life will lose it, and whoever will lose his life for My sake, and for the sake of the gospel, will save it.

36 "For what would it profit a man to gain the whole world, and forfeit his life?

37 "What should a man give in exchange for his life?

38 "For whosoever will be ashamed of Me, and of My words in this adulterous and sinful generation, the Son of Man also will be ashamed of him when He comes in the glory of His Father with the holy angels."

Feeding the Multitude

Mark 8:1-10: Man was created to be fruitful and multiply. Jesus, being the "last Adam" had authority to just bless something and it would multiply. Remember, Jesus did not come to show us how God lives—He came to show us how we are to live. God spoke and the universe came forth. We can live and show the same authority on the earth as Jesus did, if we abide in Him. In the days to come, we will need to.

Seeking a Sign from Heaven

8:11-21: In the other Gospels, we are shown that the disciples understood that Jesus was saying to beware of the teachings of the Pharisees. When Jesus used a metaphor, it was because it was comparable to what He was teaching. The teaching of the Pharisees acts like leaven. When leaven is put into dough, it creates a disturbance and puffs up the bread. The disturbance created by the legalistic teachings of the Pharisees comes because one can never measure up to a spirit of legalism, and therefore, will never find peace and rest in God through it. The puffing up is the pride that makes legalists think they are better than others. The warning here from the Son of God is not to listen to such teachings. There are times when we should leave a church or fellowship. When they start becoming legalistic is one of them.

Healing the Blind Man

8:22-26: Some prayers for healing take repetition. We may think that God can heal with one prayer, and He can, but here we see even Jesus praying more than one prayer to fully restore this man's sight. Therefore, we should not give up until the healing is complete. John G. Lake prayed for a woman for fourteen hours one time. When asked why, he just said that he prayed until he felt the compassion of the Lord released for her, and then he knew she was healed. There are many cases where people prayed for weeks or months before breakthrough. We should never give up until the Lord answers.

The Great Confession

8:27-38: In this one incident, Peter went from having one of the greatest revelations from above, to hearing from Satan. The one thing that can most set us up to hear from the devil is to set our mind on man's interests rather than God's. This is why the Lord made it clear that basic discipleship was to take up our cross daily. Nothing has so distracted people from true discipleship like the fear of man.

NOTES

THE GOSPEL OF
MARK

Mark 9

The Mount of Transfiguration

1   He said to them, "Truly I say to you, there are some who are standing here who will not taste of death until they see the kingdom of God come with power."

2   After six days Jesus took with Him Peter, James, and John, and they went apart by themselves up into a high mountain, and He was transfigured before them,

3   and His garments were glistering a brilliant white, more than any fuller on the earth could whiten them.

4   Then Elijah and Moses appeared to them, talking with Jesus.

5   Then Peter answered and said to Jesus, "Rabbi, it is good for us to be here. Let us make three tabernacles; one for You, and one for Moses, and one for Elijah."

6   He was speaking out of his fear because they were very afraid.

7   Then a cloud came and overshadowed them, and a voice came out of the cloud, saying, "This is My beloved Son. Listen to Him!"

8   Suddenly they looked around and saw no one, except for Jesus Himself, alone.

9   As they were coming down from the mountain, He charged them not to tell anyone the things they had seen until the Son of Man had risen again from the dead.

10 They kept questioning among themselves what the rising again from the dead meant.

11 So they asked Him, saying, "How is it that the scribes say that Elijah must first come?"

12 He said to them, "Elijah does indeed come first, to restore all things. And how is it written of the Son of Man, that He should suffer many things and be rejected?

13 "But I say to you that Elijah did come, and they have done to him whatever they would, even as it is written of him."

14 When they came to the other disciples, they saw a great multitude around them, and scribes were questioning them.

15 When the multitude saw Him, they were greatly amazed, and running to Him they greeted Him.

The Difficult Deliverance

16 So He asked them, "Why do you question them?"

17 One in the crowd answered Him, "Teacher, I brought my son to You who has a dumb spirit,

18 "and whenever it takes him, it casts him down, and he foams at the mouth, and grinds his teeth, and shies away. So I asked Your disciples to cast it out, and they were not able to."

19 So He answered them and said, "O faithless generation! How long must I be with you? How long must I bear with you? Bring him to Me."

20 So they brought him to Him, and when he saw Him, immediately the spirit tore him grievously, and he fell on the ground, and wallowed about while foaming.

21 So He asked his father, "How long has this been happening to him?" He answered, "Since he was a child."

22 "Sometimes it casts him into the fire, and into the water, seeking to destroy him. If You can do anything, have compassion on us, and help us."

23 Jesus said to him, "If you can? All things are possible to him that believes."

24 Immediately the father of the child cried out, and said, "I believe! Help me with my unbelief!"

25 When Jesus saw that a multitude came running together, He rebuked the unclean spirit, saying to him, "You deaf and dumb spirit, I command you to come out of him, and do not enter into him again."

26 So, having cried out, it tore him again very badly, and then he came out. Then the boy became as one dead so that most of the people said, "He is dead."

27 Then Jesus took him by the hand, and raised him up, and he stood.

28 When He had come into the house, His disciples asked Him privately, "Why could we not cast it out?"

29 He said to them, "This kind cannot come out by anything but prayer."

30 Then they went out from there, and passed through Galilee, and He desired that no one would know it.

31 Then He instructed His disciples, and said to them, "The Son of Man will be delivered into the hands of men, and they will kill Him, and after three days He will rise again."

32 However, they did not understand what He was saying, and were afraid to ask Him.

Who is the Greatest?

33 When they came to Capernaum, and when He was in the house He asked them, "What were you talking about on the way?"

34 They remained silent, because they had disputed with one another about who was the greatest among them.

35 So He sat down, and called the twelve and said to them, "If any man wants to be first, he will be last of all, and servant of all."

36 Then He took a little child, and set him in the midst of them, and taking him in His arms, He said to them,

37 "Whoever will receive one such little child in My name, receives Me. Whoever receives Me, receives not just Me, but also Him that sent Me."

38 John said to Him, "Teacher, we saw one casting out demons in Your name, and we forbid him to do it anymore, because he was not following us."

39 Jesus replied, "Do not forbid him! For there is no man who will do a work of power in My name, and then be able to soon speak evil of Me.

40 "He that is not against us is for us.

41 "Whoever will give you a cup of water to drink, because you are Christ's, truly I say to you, he will in no way lose his reward.

42 "Whoever will cause one of these little ones that believe in Me to stumble, it would be better for him if a great millstone were hung around his neck, and he was cast into the sea.

43 "If your hand causes you to stumble, cut it off. It would be better for you to enter into life maimed, rather than having your two hands to go into the Ghehenna of unquenchable fire.

44 "If your foot causes you to stumble, cut it off. It is better for you to enter into life crippled than having your two feet to be cast into Ghehenna.

45 "If your eye causes you to stumble, cast it out. It is better for you to enter into the kingdom of God with one eye, rather than having two eyes to be cast into Ghehenna,

46 "because everyone will be salted with fire.

47 "Salt is good: but if the salt has lost its saltiness, with what will it be salted? Have salt in yourselves, and be at peace with one another."

The Mount of Transfiguration

Mark 9:1-15: The transfiguration is an important revelation of Jesus. Having Moses and Elijah speak to Him is a message of how both Moses and the prophets spoke of Jesus. No one else in history had the credentials that Jesus did—having been spoken of by so many for so long, and then perfectly fulfilling the many prophecies about His life.

This revelation was not so they could each have a tabernacle built for them by man, but so that the disciples would

understand and hear from heaven that now we are to listen to the Son. When they heard this message, they looked up and "saw no one but Jesus Himself alone." This is the main point of the revelation—it is Jesus alone. We can learn from all who prepared the way for Him, but Jesus is more than a messenger—He is the Message.

The Difficult Deliverance

9:16-32: It is interesting that it seems everyone in biblical times recognized demons. However, the authority to cast them out was extraordinary, and this was a major part of the ministry of Jesus. He also made it an important part of the authority He gave to His disciples and it still is.

Some demons may be more difficult than others to cast out, as this one was, but there are none that can resist the authority of Jesus. We have His authority to the degree that we abide in Him. However, who abides in Him perfectly? This is something we grow into, and as we are growing, there will be demons we encounter that will require more authority and faith, and we will need additional prayer.

Some translations add the words "and fasting" to verse 29, but these words are not in the earliest manuscripts.

Who is the Greatest?

9:33-47: Horses are made geldings to make them more peaceful and less prone to compete in a herd. This works to help keep the peace, but geldings cannot reproduce. The Lord chose leaders who were spiritual stallions. Though they may fight more among themselves, they reproduce their ministry in many others. The Lord did not rebuke them for their debate over who was the greatest, as it is the nature of great leaders to be greatly competitive. But He taught them how to become the greatest.

As the Lord taught here, the most basic way to become greater in spiritual authority is to become like a child. God gives

His grace to the humble, and children have one of the greatest aspects of humility—they are teachable.

The Lord said as we treat even the least of His, it would be counted as having been done for Him. Now think about what we can do for Him today by doing something for one of His people. What kind of society would it be if everyone was constantly serving each other, knowing that as they did this it would be counted as if they had served the Lord Himself? This is what the kingdom is like. We can live in it now by serving one another.

Ghehenna was a valley outside of Jerusalem where the trash from the city was burned. This fire was kept going perpetually. This made it the symbol for hell in the Middle Ages and became the basis for the doctrines for the eternal burning in hell that sinners would suffer. There are other Scriptures that seem to support this concept. However, it was not a concept that any of the first apostles or early church fathers mentioned in their extensive writings, and does not appear until centuries later in the modern form that is accepted today. The penalty for sin is death, according to Scripture, and death is defined in Scripture as returning to the dust from which we came, which is effectively ceasing to exist; others assert that the fire of Ghehenna itself burns eternally, but not the individual pieces of trash thrown into it—the trash is consumed and ceases to exist. Whether hell is a place of eternal fire or whether a lost soul ceases to exist is a controversy that has much more to it, and both sides have obvious merit to their position.

As the Lord asserts here, causing even one of His people to stumble is one of the worst things we could do. Those who have children understand this. What would we feel about the one who did something that greatly hurt one of our children?

NOTES

THE GOSPEL OF
MARK

Mark 10

The Question of Divorce

1 He arose from there and came to the borders of Judea beyond the Jordan where multitudes came to Him again. As He was prone to do, He taught them.

2 Pharisees then came to Him asking, "Is it lawful for a man to put away his wife?" This they asked in order to test Him.

3 He answered and said to them, "What did Moses command you?"

4 They replied, "Moses allowed us to write a certificate of divorce, and to put her away" (see Deuteronomy 24:1-4).

5 Jesus then said to them, "It was because of the hardness of your heart that he wrote this commandment.

6 **"From the beginning of the creation He made them male and female** (see Genesis 1:27, 5:2).

7 **"For this cause shall a man leave his father and mother, and shall cleave to his wife;**

8 **"and the two shall become one flesh: so that they are no more two, but one flesh** (see Genesis 2:24).

9 "What therefore God has joined together, let no man put asunder."

10 Later, when in the house, the disciples asked Him again about this matter.

11 He said to them, "Whoever shall put away his wife, and marry another, commits adultery against her.

12 "If she herself shall put away her husband, and marry another, she commits adultery."

Let Children Come to Him

13 They were bringing to Him little children so that He could touch them, and the disciples rebuked them.

14 When Jesus saw it, He was moved with indignation, and said to them, "Allow the little children to come to Me! Do not forbid them, because it is to such as these that the kingdom of God belongs.

15 "Truly I say to you, whoever will not receive the kingdom of God as a little child, will in no way enter it."

16 So He took them in His arms, and blessed them, laying His hands upon them.

The Rich Young Ruler

17 As He was going forth a man ran up to Him, and kneeling before Him, asked, "Good Teacher, what must I do that I may inherit eternal life?"

18 Jesus replied to him, "Why do you call Me good? There is none good except One, even God.

19 "You know the commandments, **'Do not kill, Do not commit adultery, Do not steal, Do not bear false witness, Do not defraud, Honor your father and mother'**" (see Exodus 20:12-16).

20 So he replied to Him, "Teacher, all these things I have observed from my youth."

21 Jesus looking upon him loved him, and said, "One thing you lack. Go, sell whatever you have, and give it to the poor, and you will have treasure in heaven. Then come, follow Me."

22 Then his countenance fell when he heard this, and he went away sorrowful, because he was one that had great possessions.

23 Jesus then looked round about, and said to His disciples, "How hard it is for those who have riches to enter the kingdom of God!"

24 The disciples were amazed at His words. Jesus repeated it to them, saying, "Children, how hard it is for those who trust in riches to enter into the kingdom of God!

25 "It is easier for a camel to go through the eye of a needle than for a rich man to enter into the kingdom of God."

26 So they were amazed, saying to Him, "Then who can be saved?"

27 Jesus looking upon them said, "With men it is impossible, but not with God, because all things are possible with God."

28 Peter began to say to Him, "Lord, we have left all, and have followed You."

29 Jesus said, "Truly, truly I say to you, there is no man that has left house, or brothers, or sisters, or mother, or father, or children, or lands, for My sake, and for the gospel's sake,

30 "who will not receive a hundredfold now, in this age, houses, and brothers, and sisters, and mothers, and children, and lands, along with persecutions, and in the age to come, eternal life.

31 "But many that are first will be last, and the last first."

Facing the Cross

32 They were going up to Jerusalem, and Jesus was going before them, and they were amazed that He was doing this, and they that followed were afraid. So He took aside the twelve, and began to tell them again the things that were going to happen to Him,

33 (saying), "Behold, we are going up to Jerusalem, and the Son of Man will be delivered to the chief priests and the scribes, and they will condemn Him to death, and will deliver Him to the Gentiles.

34 "They will mock Him, and will spit upon Him, and will scourge Him, and will kill Him, but after three days He will rise again."

Kingdom Authority

35 James and John, the sons of Zebedee, drew near to Him, saying, "Teacher, we would like for You to do for us whatever we ask of You."

36 He said to them, "What do you want Me to do for you?"

37 They said to Him, "Grant to us that we may sit, one on Your right hand, and one on Your left hand, in Your glory."

38 Jesus then said to them, "You do not know what you are asking. Are you able to drink the cup that I drink? Or to be baptized with the baptism that I am baptized with?"

39 They said to Him, "We are able." Then Jesus said to them, "The cup that I drink you shall drink, and with the baptism that I am baptized with shall you be baptized,

40 "but to sit on My right hand or on My left hand is not Mine to give, but it is for those for whom it has been prepared."

41 When the other ten disciples heard it they were indignant with James and John.

42 So Jesus called them to Himself, and said, "You know that they who rule over the Gentiles lord it over them, and their great ones exercise authority over them.

43 "It is not to be that way with you. Whoever would become great among you will be your servant,

44 "and whoever would be first among you will be the servant of all.

45 "For the Son of Man did not come to be served, but to serve, and to give His life a ransom for many."

The Blind Beggar

46 Then they came to Jericho, and as He went out from Jericho with His disciples and a great multitude, the son of Timaeus, Bartimaeus, a blind beggar, was sitting by the side of the road.

47 When he heard that it was Jesus the Nazarene, he began to cry out, and say, "Jesus, Son of David, have mercy on me."

48 Many rebuked him, telling him to be quiet, but he cried out even more, "Son of David, have mercy on me."

49 Jesus stopped, and said, "Call him over." So they called the blind man, saying to him, "Be of good cheer! Rise, He is calling for you."

50 Casting away his garment, he sprang up, and came to Jesus.

51 Jesus said to him, "What would you have Me to do for you?" The blind man said to Him, "Rabbi, I want to receive my sight."

52 Jesus then said to him, "Go your way; your faith has made you whole." Immediately he received his sight, and followed Him on the road.

The Question of Divorce

Mark 10:1-12: Many English translations mistranslate this text in a way that makes it confusing. This has led to the implementation of a devastating doctrine in much of the church. We know that the Lord said that He did not come to change the law, and the law is very clear on the matter of divorce. It does allow divorce, and an accurate translation of this text verifies this.

An Orthodox Jewish Rabbi, who is a believer in Jesus as the Messiah, pointed out to me that in the Lord's time, many in Israel, especially among the Pharisees, were putting away their wives without giving them a certificate of divorce, as the law required. This condemned the ones put out to never be able to remarry because they were technically still married. If either party married again without the divorce being made official by the certificate, then both would be committing adultery. This practice of not giving the certificate of divorce was what the Lord was condemning here. The accuracy of this is confirmed by the fact that the Greek word translated "put away" here is not the same word that is used for "divorce," which was a legal term.

Even though divorce is allowed, it is a defeat and a tragedy that God hates. It is always caused by a hardness of heart on the part of at least one. There are also consequences for breaking our vows, but divorce must be allowed in the church or worse consequences will result.

Presently, about half of all adult Christians are divorced. We now have almost the same percentage of Christians who no longer attend a local church. When asked why, many cite their church's doctrine of divorce by which they feel condemned.

This is already a huge loss for the body of Christ, not to mention for those who have been separated from it because of this wrong doctrine of divorce. Divorce is a tragedy. However, it is not beyond the power of the cross to heal, and that healing must come through His body.

Of course, many assert that even if this is so, removing this restraint and allowing divorce in the church would cause even more divorce. The opposite is true. Legalism is never the answer to lawlessness. The law actually empowers sin as the Apostle Paul wrote to the Corinthians. The following is clear evidence of how this is so, especially in regard to divorce.

The divorce rate among even the most conservative Christian groups that do not allow divorce is now about fifty percent. Orthodox Jews allow divorce because it is in the law, but their divorce rate is about one tenth of what it is for Christians. Why? They have found a way to brilliantly use their allowance of divorce to reconcile marriages that are headed toward divorce.

The way the Orthodox Jews do this is through the procedure a couple must go through to get a divorce. First the divorce must be granted by the rabbi who married them. The rabbi takes them through a process for the divorce, seeking any possible way of reconciliation, including such things as requiring them to read all of the biblical consequences for breaking their vows, etc. Through this process, almost every marriage is reconciled and strengthened instead of lost.

This could not happen if the couple seeking a divorce could not go to their own rabbi for the divorce, but had to go to a divorce lawyer like Christians do whose churches do not allow divorce. Paul wrote to the Corinthians that it was "to their shame" that they did not have any judges among them, but they had to go to the heathen for justice. Possibly, the number one reason that Christians go before secular judges today is for divorce. This has brought much shame to the body of Christ.

Again, legalism is never the answer to lawlessness. This teaching that a Christian cannot get a divorce is likely causing far more divorces than we would otherwise have with a truly biblical practice for this issue.

Let Children Come to Him

10:13-16: A terrible mistake many churches make is to have a program for children that is basically babysitting them while their parents are in services. Even young children can and should have their own relationship with the Lord. They can know their own calling and purpose at a very young age. Every opportunity to help teach and train them up in the Lord should be used, especially when they are children.

The Rich Young Ruler

10:17-31: The rich can enter the kingdom of God because all things are possible with God. However, Jesus is making the point that it is more difficult for those who have many possessions. This is often demonstrated by those who have a vision for making great wealth in order to use it for the kingdom. Having accomplished their goal of making great wealth, it is rare to see them actually using it for the kingdom. Having many possessions may be the primary reason why so many believers in the West seem to have a conversion experience, and may faithfully go to church and do some things for Christ, but never really live the life of a true disciple of Christ. The cares and worries of this world steal the potential fruit of many.

Then we have the historic examples of those like Count Zinzendorf, the father of the modern Moravian movement. He may have been one of the wealthiest men in the world during his time, but he expended his great fortune on the gospel so that historians have called him "the rich young ruler who said 'yes.'"

As the Lord promised, those who give up things for the sake of His kingdom will receive many times as much in this life, and much more in eternal life.

Facing the Cross

10:32-34: Jesus resolutely set His face to go to the cross and to endure its shame. To be His disciple, we must do the same, daily.

Kingdom Authority

10:35-45: Those who are well-known in heaven are likely to be little known on earth. Those who may be well-known on earth are likely to be less known in heaven, because of the truth of this text.

The Blind Beggar

10:46-52: We are repeatedly shown in the gospels how persistence with God will pay off.

NOTE

THE GOSPEL OF
MARK

Mark 11

Entering Jerusalem

1   When they came close to Jerusalem, to Bethphage and Bethany, at the Mount of Olives, He sent two of His disciples,

2   and said to them, "Go into the village next to you, and immediately when you enter it you will find a colt tied up, upon which no man has ever sat. Loose him, and bring him.

3   "If any one says to you, 'Why do you do this?' Say to them, 'The Lord has need of him.' Immediately he will send him with you."

4   So they went and found a colt tied at the door that was open to the street, and they loosed him.

5   Some who stood by said to them, "What are you doing losing the colt?"

6   They replied to them just as Jesus had told them to, and they let them go.

7   They brought the colt to Jesus, and cast their garments on it, and then He sat upon it.

8   Many others spread their garments upon the street, and others laid down branches they had cut from the fields.

9   Those who went before Him, and they that followed, cried, "Hosanna! Blessed is He that comes in the name of the Lord.

10 "Blessed is the kingdom that comes, the kingdom of our father David. Hosanna in the highest!"

11 In this way He entered into Jerusalem, and came to the temple. After He looked all around it, being evening, He went out to Bethany with the twelve.

The Fig Tree

12 On the next day, when they were coming out from Bethany, He was hungry.

13 Seeing a fig tree in the distance that had leaves, He came to it seeking to find fruit on it, but He found nothing but leaves because it was not the season for figs.

14 He said to it, "No man will ever eat fruit from you again." And His disciples heard it.

Casting Out the Money Changers

15 Then they came to Jerusalem, and He entered into the temple, and began to cast out the merchants that bought and sold in the temple, and overthrew the tables of the money-changers, and the seats of those who sold the doves.

16 So He would not allow any man to carry a vessel through the temple,

17 saying to them, "Is it not written, '**My house shall be called a house of prayer for all the nations?'** (see Isaiah 56:7; Jeremiah 7:11), but you have made it a den of robbers!"

18 The chief priests and the scribes heard it, and sought ways to destroy Him, because they feared Him, and the whole multitude was astonished at His teaching.

19 Every evening He went out of the city.

20 As they passed by in the morning, they saw the fig tree withered away from the roots.

21 So Peter said to Him, "Rabbi, behold, the fig tree that You cursed has withered away."

The Power of Faith

22 Jesus replied to them, "Have faith in God.

23 "Truly I say to you that whoever will say to this mountain, 'Be taken up and cast into the sea,' and will not doubt in his heart, but will believe that what he says will come to pass, it will be done for him.

24 "Therefore I say to you, all things that you pray and ask for, believe that you will receive them, and you will receive them.

25 "Whenever you stand praying, forgive, if you have anything against any one, so that your Father who is in heaven may forgive you of your trespasses.

26 "But if you do not forgive, neither will your Father who is in heaven forgive your trespasses."

His Authority

27 So they came again to Jerusalem, and as He was walking in the temple the chief priests came to Him, with the scribes, and the elders,

28 and they said to Him, "By what authority do you do these things? Who gave you this authority?"

29 Jesus said to them, "I will ask of you one question, and *if you* answer Me and I will tell you by what authority I do these things.

30 "The baptism of John, was it from heaven, or from men?"

31 They reasoned among themselves, saying, "If we say, 'From heaven.' He will say, 'Why then did you not believe him?'

32 "But if we say, 'From men,' we fear the people, for all held John to be a true prophet."

33 So they answered Jesus and said, "We do not know." Jesus then said to them, "Neither will I tell you by what authority I do these things."

Entering Jerusalem

Mark 11:1-11: Jesus entering Jerusalem on a donkey instead of a stallion was a statement of how He was coming at that time—in humility, as a servant and a sacrificial lamb. He will come on a stallion next time. Even though He rode a donkey, the people still recognized Him as the coming King and could not see Him as the Lamb that was about to be slain.

Jesus entered Jerusalem five days before the Passover Feast. This was the very day that all of Jerusalem and Israel were to take the lambs into their houses that they would sacrifice for the Passover. During those five days, they were to examine the lamb carefully to be sure it had no flaw. This is also what was to happen to Jesus for the next five days. He was challenged continually to try to find fault in Him, and because they could find no flaw in Him, they would hire false witnesses to accuse Him so they could kill Him. Jesus was then crucified on the day that all of Israel was to kill their Passover lambs for the feast. The Passover Lamb hung on the cross dying at the time of the evening sacrifice—the very time when all the typical lambs were being slain for the feast. Jesus, our Passover, perfectly fulfilled the prophecy that the Passover Feast was to be, and He did it right on time. He is always on time.

Even though the people's recognition and devotion to Jesus was appropriate here, it was nevertheless shallow. Just five days later, the same crowd would be crying "Crucify Him!" Today politicians determine their decisions by how it will play out politically, how the people will feel about it. That is the difference between a politician and a leader. Jesus was the ultimate leader—the King of kings. He got His authority from above, not below. As Paul the apostle said in Galatians 1:10: "If I were still seeking to please men I would not be a bondservant of Christ." That is the resolve of all who truly follow Him.

The Fig Tree

11:12-14: The lesson of the fig tree is that it is a serious matter not to bear fruit for the Lord when He expects it. As we are told in John 15, those who do not bear fruit will be cut off. We are on the earth for this purpose, and bearing fruit is evidence that we are abiding in the Lord. As we are taught by this lesson too, He expects fruit in every season of our life.

Casting Out the Money Changers

11:15-21: Jesus could not help but to care about His Father's house. All who are abiding in Him will likewise have a deep concern for His house, which is now the church. The Lord's house is not meant to be just a house of merchandise. We must be careful that our resources and products are for serving the house of God and not for using the house of God to serve us.

The Power of Faith

11:22-26: Before the end of this age, it will be demonstrated that this word is true as believers will say to literal mountains, "Be plucked up and cast into the sea," and it will be done. This is a small thing for the Lord who cast out the stars like a tent curtain, but they are big for us. Even so, the best has been saved for last. His greatest works will be done through His people at the end of the age.

We should also note here how the Lord linked forgiveness to this kind of faith. The most successful in any field are those who do the basics best. So it is with our faith as well. If we would have the authority to move mountains, then we must never forget the basics of the faith: to love and forgive.

His Authority

11:27-33: Jesus had an authority greater than any other because He was sent by the Father. As we see in the Gospel of John, Colossians, and Hebrews, Jesus was also the One through whom the world was created. Most would think that He would have answered this question by declaring this, but He did not. He pointed to the baptism of John as the basis of His earthly authority. John was the last of an order that had all prophesied of Him and prepared the way for Him over many centuries. John was there to represent that order, to point to Jesus and say that He was the One they had all been speaking of. Then Jesus fulfilled all of the prophecies they had spoken of Him. No one in history has had those credentials. If you understood who John was, you know who Jesus is.

NOTES

The Gospel of
MARK
Mark 12

Parable of the Vineyard

1 Then He began to speak to them again in parables, saying: "A man planted a vineyard, and set a hedge about it. Then he dug a pit for the winepress, and built a tower. After this he rented it out to husbandmen, and went on a journey into another country.

2 "At the season he sent to the husbandmen a servant, so that he might receive from them the profits from the vineyard.

3 "They took him, and beat him, and sent him away empty.

4 "Again he sent to them another servant, and they wounded him in the head, and handled him shamefully.

5 "So he sent another, and they killed him. So he sent many others, and they beat some, and killed some.

6 "He had yet one, a beloved son, which he sent to them at the last, saying, 'They will revere my son.'

7 "But those husbandmen reasoned among themselves, 'This is the heir. Come, let us kill him, and the inheritance will be ours.'

8 "So they took him, and killed him, and cast him out of the vineyard.

9 "What therefore will the lord of the vineyard do? He will come and destroy the husbandmen, and will give the vineyard to others.

10 "Have you not read even this Scripture, **'The stone which the builders rejected, the same was made the chief cornerstone;**

11 **'This was from the Lord, and it is marvelous in our eyes?'"** (see Psalm 118:22-23)

12 Then they sought to capture Him, because they perceived that He spoke this parable about them, but they feared the multitude, and so they left Him, and went away.

Paying Taxes

13 Then they sent certain of the Pharisees to Him, and some of the Herodians, that they might catch Him in what He said.

14 When they had come, they said to Him, "Teacher, we know that You are true, and do not care what others think, because You do not fear men, but teach the way of God without compromise. Therefore, is it lawful to give tribute to Caesar, or not?

15 "Should we give, or should we not give this tribute?" Knowing their hypocrisy, He said to them, "Why do you test Me? Bring Me a denarius so I can see it."

16 So they brought it. He then said to them, "Whose image and inscription is on this?" They answered Him, "Caesar's."

17 So Jesus said to them, "Render to Caesar the things that are Caesar's, and to God the things that are God's." Then they marveled greatly at Him.

Marriage in the Resurrection

18 Then Sadducees came to Him who say that there is no resurrection, and they asked Him, saying,

19 "Teacher, Moses wrote to us that if a man's brother dies, and leaves a wife behind, and leaves no child, that his brother should take his wife, and raise up seed for his brother.

20 "There were seven brethren, and the first took a wife, and died without leaving her with a child.

21 "So the second took her, and died, leaving no child. The third did likewise,

22 "until all seven left no seed. Last of all, the woman also died.

23 "In the resurrection, whose wife shall she be, for all seven had her as a wife?"

24 Jesus said to them, "You err because you do not know the Scriptures nor the power of God."

25 "When they rise from the dead they neither marry, nor are given in marriage, but are like angels in heaven."

26 "Concerning the dead, and the fact that they are raised, have you not read in the book of Moses, how God spoke to him from the bush, saying, '**I am the God of Abraham, and the God of Isaac, and the God of Jacob?'** (see Exodus 3:2-6)

27 "He is not the God of the dead, but of the living. You are in great error."

The Greatest Commandment

28 One of the scribes came, and heard them questioning together, and knowing that He had answered them all well, asked Him, "What commandment is the first of all?"

29 Jesus answered, "The first is, '**Hear, O Israel; The Lord our God, The Lord is one:**

30 "'**and you shall love the Lord your God with all of your heart, and with all of your soul, and with all of your mind, and with all of your strength**' (see Deuteronomy 6:4-5).

31 "The second is this, 'You shall love your neighbor as yourself.' (see Leviticus 19:18). There is no other commandment greater than these."

32 Then the scribe said to Him, "This is truth, Teacher. You have said it well. He is one, and there is no other God but Him.

33 "To love Him with all of our heart, and with all of our understanding, and with all of our strength, and to love our neighbor as ourselves, is much better than all whole burnt offerings and sacrifices."

34 When Jesus saw that he answered so discreetly, He said to him, "You are not far from the kingdom of God." After this no man after that dared to ask Him a question.

35 Then Jesus, as He taught in the temple, asked "How do the scribes say that the Christ is the son of David?

36 "David himself said by the Holy Spirit, **'The Lord said to my Lord, "'Sit at My right hand until I make your enemies a footstool for Your feet'"** (see Psalm110:1).

37 "David himself called Him Lord, and so how was He his son?" The common people heard Him gladly.

38 So in His teaching He said to them, "Beware of the scribes who desire to walk around in long robes, and to have salutations in the marketplaces,

39 "and chief seats in the synagogues, and chief places at feasts.

40 "They are the ones that devour widows' houses, and for a pretense make long prayers, but these will receive a greater condemnation."

The Great Offering

41 Then He sat down over by the treasury, and beheld how the multitude cast money into the treasury, and many that were rich cast in much.

42 There came a poor widow, and she cast in two small copper coins which together only made a penny.

43 He called His disciples to Himself, and said to them, "Truly I say to you, this poor widow cast in more than all they that are casting into the treasury,

44 "because they all gave from their abundance, but she gave even while in great need, and cast in all that she had, even that she had to live on."

Parable of the Vineyard

Mark 12:1-12: The chief priests perceived that He had spoken this parable about them, and they were right. With a few exceptions in their history, the leaders of Israel had killed, or at least mistreated, virtually all of the messengers the Lord had sent to them. Finally they were going to reject and kill His Son. Even so, the Lord loves them, still to this day, and reaches out to them.

Israel is a prophetic parallel of all mankind in some ways, a spiritual barometer that reflects the general state of mankind. With their behavior, we have a very close parallel of the way mankind has rejected the Lord. Even so, He still loves us and reaches out to us. As the prophets concur, there will be a time when all Israel will be saved and all mankind will repent and turn to Him.

If this is the patience with which the Lord has treated us, should we not have this same patience with one another?

Paying Taxes

12:13-17: There are Christians who debate whether they should pay taxes, especially to unrighteous governments that use resources to do unrighteousness. The text here and other Scriptures concur that we are to obey the civil authorities, except when they command us to do what is in violation of God's Word. God will ultimately hold them responsible for what they do with our taxes, but we are commanded to pay our taxes. Even so, the main purpose of this is the responsibility to know the things that are God's and the things that belong to the world, and give to God what is His.

Marriage in the Resurrection

12:18-27: Verse 24 is a key to not only understanding this discourse, but all of them, and to understand the will of God in general. Many know the Scriptures well, but because they do not know God's power, they have error in their doctrine. Others know His power but do not know His Scriptures well, so they also fall into error. The strongest Christians, churches, and movements are those devoted to knowing both the Scriptures and the power of God.

The Greatest Commandment

12:28-40: Jesus also said that these two commandments fulfill the whole law. If we keep these two, we will fulfill the law.

If we love God above all things, we will not worship idols. If we love our neighbors, we will not steal from them, envy what is theirs, or murder them. So love fulfills the law. The single factor that will determine how successful we have been in this life will be how much we have loved.

The Great Offering

12:41-44: The greatest faith, and one of the greatest opportunities to bless the Lord who is pleased by our faith, is to give extravagantly when we are going through the most difficult times financially. To give when we are in need is an opportunity to bless the Lord that we do not want to miss. When people ask me to bless them so they can be a blessing to the kingdom, I tell them they can be the greatest blessing before they are blessed with abundance. Those who are not generous when they are in need are not likely to be generous when they have abundance either. I have seen many blessed financially as they requested, but then they do not follow up with the generosity they said they would have. This is such an affront to the Lord that it would be better not to be blessed in this way.

The Apostle Paul said that he learned to be content in whatever state he was in, whether abounding or in need. We must do the same because virtually all people go through such ups and downs. We must consider what God's purpose is first. Then we must resolve to have faith whether we are abounding or in need. Faith is not just for the good or bad times, but for all time.

NOTES

THE GOSPEL OF
MARK
Mark 13

The Signs of the End of the Age

1   As He left the temple, one of His disciples said to Him, "Teacher, behold, what amazing stone works and buildings!"

2   Jesus said to him, "See these great buildings? There will not be left here one stone upon another that will not be thrown down."

3   As He sat on the Mount of Olives opposite the temple, Peter and James and John and Andrew questioned Him privately,

4   "Tell us, when will these things be? What will be the sign when these things are all about to come to pass?"

5   Jesus began to instruct them, "Take heed that no man leads you astray.

6   "Many will come in My name, saying that I am the Christ, and yet will lead many astray.

7   "When you hear of wars and rumors of wars, do not be troubled. These things must come to pass, but that does not mean that it is the end.

8   "For ethnic groups will rise against other ethnic groups, nations and kingdoms will war against each other. There will be earthquakes in different places, and famines, but these are just the beginning of travail.

9   "Take heed to yourselves, for they will deliver you up to councils, and in synagogues you will be beaten, and you will be brought before governors and kings to take your stand for My sake for a testimony to them,

10 "because the gospel must first be preached to all nations.

11 "So when they lead you to court, and deliver you up, do not be anxious beforehand as to what you will speak, but it will be given to you in that hour what you will speak. For it is not you that will speak, but the Holy Spirit will speak through you.

12 "Brother will betray brother to death, and a father his child. Children will rise up against their parents, and cause them to be put to death.

13 "You will be hated by all men for My name's sake, but he that endures to the end will be saved.

14 "When you see the abomination of desolation standing where it should not stand (let him that reads understand), then let those who are in Judea flee to the mountains.

15 "Let he who is on the housetop not go down, nor enter in to their house to take anything out.

16 "Let the one that is in the field not return back for his cloak.

17 "Woe to those who are with child, and to those who nurse babes in those days!

18 "Pray that it is not in the winter.

19 "For in those days there will be tribulation such as there has not been from the beginning of the creation until now, and never will be again.

20 "Except the Lord had shortened those days, no flesh would have been saved. However, for the elect's sake, whom He chose, He will shorten the days.

21 "Then if any man will say to you, 'Behold, here is the Christ'; or, 'Behold, He is over there'; do not believe it.

22 "False Christs will arise, along with false prophets, and they will show signs and wonders so that they may lead astray, if possible, even the elect.

23 "Take heed that I have told you all these things beforehand.

24 "In those days, after the tribulation, the sun will be darkened, and the moon will not give her light,

25 "and the stars will be falling from heaven, and the powers that are in the heavens will be shaken.

26 "Then they will see the Son of Man coming in clouds with great power and glory.

27 "Then He will send forth the angels, and will gather together His elect from the four winds, from the uttermost part of the earth to the uttermost part of heaven.

28 "Now learn the parable of the fig tree: when her branch has become tender, and puts forth its leaves, you know that the summer is near.

29 "In this same way, you also, when you see these things coming to pass, know that He is close, even at the door.

30 "Truly I say to you, this race of people will not pass away until all of these things have taken place.

31 "Heaven and earth will pass away, but My words will not pass away.

32 "However, the day or the hour no one knows, not even the angels in heaven, not even the Son, but only the Father.

33 "Take heed to watch and pray, for you do not know when the time is.

34 "It is as when a man, sojourning in another country, having left his house, and given authority to his servants for each one to do his work, and he commanded the porter also to keep watch,

36 "lest coming suddenly, He finds you sleeping.

37 "What I say to you I say to all, Watch!"

The Signs of the End of the Age

Mark 13:1-37: There are three basic schools of interpretation about this prophecy and the end of the age. The first maintains that this entire prophecy was about the invasion of Israel by the Roman General Titus in 70 A.D. These interpret the "end of the age" to be the end of the Jewish age in which the Lord dealt almost exclusively with the Jewish people. Much of this does obviously apply in this way, such as the temple being destroyed and the people having to flee to the mountains. However, some of this prophecy was not fulfilled then, such as the Lord's return.

The next view is also a historical one that sees this prophecy being fulfilled in history beginning with the invasion of Titus and extending through the period leading to this time. There are many ways in which events in history match what the Lord foretold here as well as the other biblical prophecies regarding the end of the age, such as we find in the Books of Daniel and Revelation. Even so, the big one—the Lord's return—has not yet happened.

The last view interprets this prophecy, as well as most of the other biblical prophecies and prophetic books such as Daniel and Revelation, to be almost exclusively about the very end of the age.

There is some merit to each of these views. Certainly the part about the temple was fulfilled with Titus' invasion. Much of the rest of this prophecy was seemingly fulfilled by events over the nearly two thousand years since it was given. Because the question to the Lord was about the end of the age, it is understandable that some would consider it all to be about the end times. However, the early church fathers interpreted the end of this age to last about two thousand years, which was stated very directly in some of their writings. How they concluded this is interesting and worth taking a few minutes to understand.

First, the early church fathers were the direct disciples of the first apostles. For example, Irenaeus was Peter's disciple, Polycarp was John's, and so forth. Some of the early church fathers wrote more extensively than the apostles. Though their writings have never been considered canon Scripture, having been the direct disciples of those who walked with the Lord and wrote the New Testament, their writings are given great credibility in verifying what the apostles taught. Their writings do address the prophecy above and others about the end times.

One important aspect that seemed to be consistent with the early church fathers is that they saw biblical prophecy being fulfilled over a seven thousand year period from Adam. If you take the genealogies of Scripture and add them up, man has now been on the earth about six thousand years. As we are told in II Peter 3:8:

"Do not let this one fact escape your notice, beloved, that with the Lord one day is as a thousand years, and a thousand years is as one day."

To the early church fathers, this meant that the end of this age would come about six thousand years from the creation of Adam or over six prophetic one-thousand-year days. When the Lord said that He was "the Lord of the Sabbath," He was not talking about being Lord just one day a week, but that He would rule on the Sabbath of this prophetic week—the last one thousand year period, also called "the millennium." When they wrote and spoke of "the last days," they were speaking of the last two days of this prophetic week—the last two thousand years. This is stated clearly in some of the early writings such as The Epistle of Barnabas:

"And God made in six days the works of His hands; and He finished them on the seventh day, and He rested the seventh day and sanctified it.

"Consider, my children, what that signifies. He finished them in six days. The meaning of it is this: that in six thousand years the Lord God will bring all things to an end.

"For with Him one day is a thousand years; and He Himself testifies, saying, 'Behold this day shall be as a thousand years'. Therefore, children, in six days, that is, in six thousand years, shall all things be accomplished" (13:2-5).

The Epistle of Barnabas is controversial with some, and some continue to think that it should have been canonized. The main reason it was not canonized is because its message was considered redundant to the other New Testament writings, but it is generally agreed that it is the authentic writing of

Barnabas, the associate of the Apostle Paul. This epistle, along with the writings of the early church fathers, does not conflict with any of the teachings of the writings that were canonized, but it does conflict with some things that are popular eschatology today.

The point of the Lord's discourse here is the end of the age, which obviously is near according to any interpretation. The reason He gave this prophecy was so that we could be prepared for this time. I interpret verse 17 as, "Woe to those who keep their people in immaturity." We are obviously getting close to these times, and we must be prepared for them. The greatest preparation is spiritual maturity.

For those who hold to the pre-tribulation rapture doctrine, this text presents a number of problems. In verse 24, we see these things happening "after the tribulation." In verses 26-27, we see that it is when the Lord is seen coming in His glory that He gathers His elect from the earth. An obvious problem of the pre-tribulation doctrine is that it requires a second and then a third coming of Christ, first to take His people out before the tribulation and then another coming after the tribulation.

There are other texts that seem to conflict with a pre-tribulation doctrine that will be covered as they come. Even so, we know there will be what is now called the "rapture" of the faithful. We do know for sure there will be a time when the Lord comes with His saints and catches up His people who remain on the earth at that time. As we are commanded here, and many other places in Scripture, we are to watch and be awake until He comes. About that, we should all be able to agree.

One reason why this chapter in Mark, Matthew 24, and others can get confusing is because people fail to understand that the disciples asked the Lord three different questions about three different events, and the Lord addresses all three. This is more clearly seen in Matthew, but the three questions were:

1) When will these things be (the temple destroyed)?

2) What are the signs of the end of the age?

3) What are the signs of His coming again?

In this discourse, the Lord answers all three of these questions, and as is typical of biblical prophecies, He is not necessarily answering them in the sequence in which they were to take place. One of the reasons why so many biblical prophecies have been misunderstood or misinterpreted is because people took them in sequence when the Lord had obviously and purposely jumbled the sequence.

Why would the Lord jumble the sequence of prophecies? The interpretation and understanding are only for those who are taught of the Holy Spirit, not those who seek to understand them just by their own reasoning or by some scientific or mathematical method.

NOTES

THE GOSPEL OF
MARK

Mark 14

Anointed for Burial

1 Now after two days it was the Feast of the Passover and Unleavened Bread, and the chief priests and the scribes were seeking ways to take Him secretly, and kill Him.

2 However, they said, "Not during the feast, lest there would be a riot among the people."

3 While He was in Bethany in the house of Simon the leper, as He sat at His meal, a woman came who had an alabaster cruse of pure and very costly ointment. She broke the cruse, and poured it over His head.

4 There were some that became indignant at this, saying, "To what purpose has this ointment been wasted?

5 "This ointment might have been sold for more than three hundred denarii to be given to the poor." So they grumbled against her.

6 Jesus then said, "Let her alone. Why do you trouble her? She has done a good deed for Me.

7 "For the poor you will always have with you, and whenever you want you can do good for them, but you will not always have Me.

8 "She has done what she could, and she has anointed My body beforehand for My burial.

9 "Truly I say to you, wherever the gospel is preached throughout the whole world what this woman has done will be told for a memorial to her."

The Betrayal

10 Then Judas Iscariot, who was one of the twelve, went to the chief priests and offered to deliver Him to them.

11 When they heard it, they were glad, and promised to give him money. So he sought a way to conveniently betray Him into their hands.

12 On the first day of Unleavened Bread, when they sacrificed the Passover, His disciples said to Him, "Where do You want us to go and prepare for You to eat the Passover?"

13 He sent two of His disciples, and said to them, "Go into the city, and there you will meet a man bearing a pitcher of water. Follow him,

14 "and where he enters, say to the master of the house, 'The Teacher said, "'Where is My guest-chamber where I can eat the Passover with My disciples?'"

15 "He will himself show you a large upper room furnished and ready, and there you can prepare it for us."

16 So the disciples went into the city, and found all just as He had said to them, and they prepared for the Passover.

17 When it was evening He came with the twelve.

18 As they sat and were eating, Jesus said, "Truly I say to you, one of you will betray Me, even the one who eats with Me."

19 Then they became sorrowful, and ask Him one by one, "Is it I?"

20 He said to them, "It is one of the twelve, the one that dips with Me in the dish.

21 "The Son of Man will go just as it is written of Him, but woe to that man by whom the Son of Man is betrayed! It would have been good for that man if he had not been born."

Communion

22 As they were eating, He took bread, and when He had blessed it, He broke it, and gave it to them, saying, "Take this, it is My body."

23 So He took a cup, and when He had given thanks, He gave it to them: and they all drank from it.

24 Then He said to them, "This is My blood of the covenant, which is poured out for many.

25 "Truly I say to you, I will not drink of the fruit of the vine again until that day when I drink it new in the kingdom of God."

26 When they had sung a hymn, they went out to the Mount of Olives.

27 Then Jesus said to them, "All of you will be offended just as it is written, **'I will smite the shepherd, and the sheep will be scattered abroad'** (see Zecheriah13:7).

28 "However, after I am raised up, I will go before you into Galilee."

29 So Peter said to Him, "Although all of the others are offended, I will not be."

30 Jesus said to him, "Truly I say to you, that today, even this night, before the cock crows tree times, you will deny Me three times."

31 So Peter replied vehemently, "If I must die with You, I will not deny You." The rest said the same thing.

Gethsemane

32 When they came to a place that was named Gethsemane, He said to His disciples, "Sit here, while I pray."

33 Then He took with Him Peter, James, and John, and began to be greatly agitated in spirit, and very troubled.

34 He said to them, "My soul is exceedingly sorrowful, even unto death. Wait here, and watch."

35 "So He went a little way beyond them, and fell on the ground, and prayed that, if it were possible, the hour might pass from Him.

36 He prayed, "Abba, Father, all things are possible to You, even to remove this cup from Me. However, not My will, but Your will be done."

37 He returned, and found them sleeping, and said to Peter, "Simon, why do you sleep? Could you not watch for just one hour?

38 "Watch and pray that you do not enter into temptation. The spirit indeed is willing, but the flesh is weak."

39 Again He went beyond them, and prayed the same things.

40 Again He returned, and found them sleeping. For their eyes were very heavy, and they did not know what to answer Him.

41 So He came the third time, and said to them, "Sleep on now, and take your rest. It is enough; the hour has come. Behold, the Son of Man is being betrayed into the hands of sinners.

42 "Arise, let us be going. The one that betrayed Me is close."

43 Immediately, while He was still speaking, Judas came, who was one of the twelve, and with him a multitude with swords and spears, from the chief priests, the scribes, and the elders.

44 Now he that betrayed Him had given them a sign, saying, "The one who I kiss, that is Him. Take Him and lead Him away safely."

45 So he came forward immediately and went up to Him, and said, "Rabbi!" Then he kissed Him.

46 So they laid hands on Him, and took Him.

47 Then one of the disciples drew his sword, and smote the servant of the high priest, and cut off his ear.

48 Jesus said to them, "Have you come out as if to arrest a robber with swords and spears to seize Me?

49 "I was daily with you in the temple teaching, and you did not take Me. But it has happened this way so that the Scriptures might be fulfilled."

50 Then His disciples all left Him, and fled.

51 A young man followed with Him, having a linen cloth cast about him, over his naked body, and they seized him,

52 but he left the linen cloth, and fled naked.

53 They then led Jesus away to the high priest. And there came together with him all the chief priests, and the elders, and the scribes.

54 Peter had followed Him from a distance, even into the court of the high priest, and he was sitting with the officers, and warming himself by the fire.

Trial Before the Chief Priests

55 Now the chief priests and the whole council sought witnesses against Jesus in order to put Him to death, but they did not find any.

56 Many bore false witness spoke against Him, but their witness did not agree with each other.

57 Then one stood up to bare false witness against Him, saying,

58 We heard Him say, "I will destroy this temple that is made with hands, and in three days I will build another made without hands."

59 Even this one did not agree with the others.

60 So the high priest stood up in their midst, and asked Jesus, "Do You not answer? What is it that these witnesses are saying against You?"

61 Even so, He held His peace and did not answer. Again the high priest asked Him, "Are You the Christ, the Son of the Blessed One?"

62 Jesus then replied, "I am. And you will see the Son of Man sitting at the right hand of Power, and coming with the clouds of heaven."

63 Then the high priest tore his clothes, and said, "What further need have we of witnesses?

64 "You have heard the blasphemy. What do you think?" So they all condemned Him to be worthy of death.

65 Some began to spit on Him, and to cover His face and hit Him, saying, "Prophesy!" The officers also hit Him.

Peter's Denial

66 As Peter was outside in the court, one of the maids of the high priest came,

67   and seeing Peter warming himself, she looked at him, and said, "You were also with the Nazarene, Jesus."

68 But he denied it, saying, "I neither know nor understand what you are talking about." So he went out to the porch, and the cock crowed.

69 Then the maid saw him again, and began to again say to those who were near, "This is one of them."

70 He again denied it. And after a little while they that stood by said to Peter, "It is true. You are one of them because you are a Galilaean."

71 But he began to curse, and to swear, "I do not know this man of whom you speak."

72 Immediately the cock crowed the second time. And Peter, remembered the word that Jesus had said to him, "Before the cock crows twice, you will deny Me three times." When he remembered he began to weep.

Anointed for Burial

Mark 14:1-9: Extravagant worship of the Lord is always appropriate. This woman's adoration of Him spilled over into what has been a memorial throughout the world and throughout the ages. What could we do for Him that would touch Him in this way? Not that we should do it so that it becomes known, but what could we do that would make worship of Him a marvel?

The Betrayal

14:10-21: Judas' betrayal of Jesus is believed by some to have been politically motivated—Judas attempting to force the Lord to take His authority as King of the Jews. He obviously did not intend for Jesus to be executed, as the remorse from this caused him to hang himself. Even so, some of the worst evil is released by such devious manipulation where we would try to force others to do what we want or think is right. This is just one way that it can be true that "the road to hell is paved with good intentions."

We must always keep in mind that the good side of the Tree of Knowledge was just as deadly as the evil side and maybe more so because it seems good. But it is a goodness based on humanism rather than the righteousness of God.

Communion

14:22-31: The communion of the bread and wine is a symbolic ritual that represents the common-union we have with Christ and through Him with one another. We need to observe the ritual in remembrance of our obligation to Him and His people, but even more so we need to have communion with Him and His people.

Here we have the Son of God, not just a prophet, telling Peter that he was going to betray Him, and Peter said it was not so. This is a remarkable pride, which was likely the reason for his fall.

Gethsemane

14:32-54: The garden scene reveals Jesus in His humanity, flawless and sinless, but still human. He felt grief and pain like anyone would at such a time. We also see His most trusted disciples—those who He, the greatest leader there would ever be, had personally trained and prepared for over three years—still weak, even to the point of not being able to stay awake for one hour to pray with Him. We are all frail indeed and would be less than worthless if it were not for Him who loves us and values us enough to pay the highest price that could be paid for our salvation—His own life. Eternity will not be long enough to thank Him.

Trial Before the Chief Priests

14:55-65: The trial of Jesus violated many of the basic laws of justice in the Law of Moses. We are told that Jesus was crucified because of envy. Envy can twist even those most devoted to the law so that they pervert it. This was their God, their Creator, the One who had given them their law and standards of justice. They used these things that He had given them against Him. Since this unjust trial, the consequences that Moses warned would come upon Israel for violating the law and the justice that God demanded be preserved for His people are now the history of the Jewish people.

Peter's Denial

14:66-72: Peter was one of the most courageous men in Scripture. He had gotten out of the boat to walk on water during a storm. This night he had drawn his sword in the face of a Roman Cohort, which numbered eight hundred men. He was no coward, but he did not recognize the source of his courage—God's grace. God resists the proud and gives grace to the humble. When Peter showed the extraordinary pride of rejecting the warning from the Son of God Himself that he would deny Him, grace was lifted. Then before morning, this man who had stood and challenged a Roman Cohort could not even stand in front of a servant girl. It is more than a cliché that if we stand at all, it is by the grace of God.

NOTES

THE GOSPEL OF
MARK

Mark 15

Trial Before Pilate

1 In the morning, the chief priests with the elders and scribes, and the whole council, quickly held a consultation. Then they bound Jesus, and carried Him away to be delivered to Pilate.

2 Pilate asked Him, "Are You the King of the Jews?" He answered and said to him, "It is as you say."

3 Then the chief priests accused Him of many things.

4 Pilate again asked Him, "Do You not answer anything? Do You not hear how many things they accuse You of?"

5 Jesus did not answer anything, so that Pilate marveled.

6 Now at the feast Pilate used to release to them one prisoner whom they asked of him.

7 There was one called Barabbas who was imprisoned for causing an insurrection that resulted in a murder.

8 So the multitude went up and began to ask him to do as was his tradition to do for them.

9 So Pilate asked them, saying, "Do you want me to release to you the King of the Jews?"

10 This was because he perceived that it was for envy that the chief priests had delivered Him up.

11 However, the chief priests stirred up the multitude, asking that he should rather release Barabbas to them.

12 So Pilate again answered and said to them, "What then shall I do to Him whom you call the King of the Jews?"

13 They cried out again, "Crucify Him!"

14 Pilate then said to them, "Why? What evil has He done?" But they cried out even more, "Crucify Him!"

15 So Pilate, wishing to appease the multitude, released to them Barabbas, and delivered Jesus to be scourged and crucified.

Jesus Tortured

16 The soldiers led Him away to the court, which is at the Praetorium, and they called together the whole cohort.

17 There they clothed Him with purple, and weaving a crown of thorns they put it on Him.

18 Then they began to salute Him, saying, "Hail, King of the Jews!"

19 They smote His head with a reed, and spat on Him, bowing their knees, mockingly worshipping Him.

20 When they had finished mocking Him, they took off the purple robe, and put His own garments back on Him. Then they led Him out to be crucified.

21 They compelled one who was passing by, Simon of Cyrene, who had come in from that country, the father of Alexander and Rufus, to go with them to bear His cross.

22 So they brought Him to the place called Golgotha, which being interpreted means, "The place of a skull."

23 Then they offered Him wine mingled with myrrh, but He refused it.

Jesus Crucified

24 They crucified Him. Then they divided His garments among themselves, casting lots for them to see what each should take.

25 It was the third hour when they crucified Him.

26 The superscription of His accusation that was written and placed over His head read, THE KING OF THE JEWS.

27 They also crucified two robbers with Him, one on each side of Him.

28 So the Scripture was fulfilled that said, **"And He was reckoned with transgressors"** (see Isaiah 53:12).

29 Those that passed by ridiculed Him, wagging their heads, and saying, "Ha! You who would destroy the temple, and build it in three days,

30 "save Yourself, and come down from the cross."

31 In like manner also the chief priests were mocking Him along with the scribes saying, "He saved others, but He cannot save Himself."

32 "Let the Christ, the King of Israel, now come down from the cross, so that we may see and believe." Even those who were crucified with Him were also reproaching Him.

33 When the sixth hour had come, there was darkness over the whole land until 3:00 pm.

34 At 3:00 pm Jesus cried out with a loud voice, "Eloi, Eloi, lama sabachthani?" which is, being interpreted, "My God, My God, why have You forsaken Me?"

35 Some of them that stood by, when they heard it, said, "Behold, He is calling for Elijah."

36 So one ran, and filling a sponge full of vinegar, put it on a reed, and gave it to Him to drink, saying, "Let us see whether Elijah will come to take Him down."

37 Then Jesus uttered a loud voice, and gave up the Spirit.

38 At that time the veil of the temple was rent in two from the top to the bottom.

39 When the centurion, who stood close to Him saw that He had given up the Spirit, he said, "Truly this man was the Son of God."

40 There were also women watching from afar, among whom were both Mary Magdalene, and Mary the mother of James the less, and the mother of Joseph, and Salome,

41 who, when He was in Galilee, followed Him, and served Him, along with many other women that came up with Him to Jerusalem.

Fulfilling the Passover Type

42 When evening had come, because it was the Day of Preparation, that is, the day before the Sabbath,

43 Joseph of Arimathea, a councilor of honorable reputation, who also himself was looking for the kingdom of God, went boldly to Pilate, and asked for the body of Jesus.

44 Pilate marveled that He was already dead, and calling the centurion to him, he asked him whether He was indeed dead.

45 When it was confirmed to him by the centurion, he granted the body to Joseph.

46 So he bought a linen cloth, and taking Him down, wound Him in the linen cloth, and laid Him in a tomb which had been hewn out of a rock, and he rolled a stone against the door of the tomb.

47 Mary Magdalene, and Mary the mother of Joseph, beheld where He was laid.

Trial Before Pilate

Mark 15:1-15: The same crowd that had cried "Hosanna" just five days before, when Jesus entered the city, was now demanding His crucifixion. Seeking to please or follow the crowd can be one of the most treacherous paths we can take. True leaders are not overly encouraged when the crowd is with them, nor are they overly discouraged when the crowd is against them. True leaders do not just follow the crowd, but they follow the Lord and their conscience. As the great Apostle Paul said in Galatians1:10, "If I was still seeking to please men I would not be a bondservant of Christ." There are few things that can disqualify us faster or cause us to depart from following Christ than seeking to please men more than pleasing God.

Jesus Tortured

15:16-23: Jesus was the most righteous man to ever walk the earth—He was the righteousness of God. The way men treated Him is a demonstration of the contempt they have for His righteousness, and therefore, Him.

When Jesus was offered wine mixed with myrrh, it was for dulling the pain of crucifixion. Jesus refused this because He was embracing the full pain of our transgressions that He was about to bear. This He did for you and me.

Jesus Crucified

15:24-41: The rending of the veil of the temple at this time is believed to be a symbol of how access to the very presence of God, represented by the Holy of Holies, was now open to all through the cross. This is certainly true, but it may also represent that God would no longer be contained in such a small place but would now come into all the world, even our daily lives.

Fulfilling the Passover Type

15:42-47: Here it states that this happened on the Day of Preparation for the Passover, which was the day the Passover lambs were slaughtered for the feast. Three o'clock in the afternoon was the time of the evening sacrifice. Jesus died at the exact time when the Passover lambs were being killed throughout Israel. Christ, our Passover, perfectly fulfilled the prophecies, and did so right on time.

Few in Israel recognized the true Passover Lamb who had just been sacrificed in their midst. Therefore, few would partake of the true Passover Lamb from among the Jews who had carried this hope for so long. Yet there was a remnant, just as there always is. These few were the most courageous and are symbolized here by Joseph of Arimathea. When most had scattered from Jesus and it looked like He had been totally defeated, Joseph took his stand with Him, even asking for His dead body to honor Him. Joseph was a member of the Sanhedrin, and what he did was no small matter. He demonstrated more courage than the disciples of Jesus demonstrated. This reveals how even among the hardened leaders of Israel there were great and noble souls who would risk all to stand for the truth, even when it was least expedient to do so. Even among the groups today that seem to be of the same spirit as the Pharisees, we will find some great and noble souls.

NOTES

THE GOSPEL OF
MARK
Mark 16

The Resurrection

1 When the Sabbath had past, Mary Magdalene, and Mary the mother of James, and Salome, bought spices, so that they might come and anoint Him.

2 Very early on the first day of the week, they came to the tomb after the sun had risen.

3 They were saying among themselves, "Who will roll away the stone from the door of the tomb for us?" because it was very large.

4 Looking up, they saw that the stone was already rolled back.

5 Then, entering into the tomb, they saw a young man sitting on the right side, arrayed in a white robe, and they were amazed.

6 He said to them, "Do not be amazed. You seek Jesus, the Nazarene, who has been crucified. He has risen. He is not here. Look at the place where they laid Him.

7 "Go now, tell His disciples, and Peter, that He will go before you into Galilee. There you will see Him, just as He said to you."

8 So they went out, fleeing from the tomb, trembling from their great astonishment that had come upon them. So they said nothing to anyone because they were so afraid.

He Appears to His Own

9 When He had risen early on the first day of the week, He appeared first to Mary Magdalene from whom He had cast out seven demons.

10 She went and told those who had been with Him, as they mourned and wept.

11 When they heard that He was alive, and had been seen by her, they did not believe it.

12 After these things He manifested Himself in another form to two of them, as they walked on their way into the country.

13 So they went and told it to the rest, but they did not believe them either.

14 Afterward He manifested Himself to the eleven as they were sitting to eat, and He chastised them for their unbelief, and hardness of heart, because they did not believe them that had seen Him after He was risen.

15 He then said to them, "Go into all the world, and preach the gospel to the whole creation.

16 "He that believes and is baptized will be saved, but he that does not believe will be judged.

17 "These signs will follow those who believe: in My name they will cast out demons, they will speak with new tongues,

18 "they will take up serpents, and if they drink any deadly thing it will not hurt them. They will lay hands on the sick, and they will recover."

19 So then the Lord Jesus, after He had spoken to them, was received up into heaven, and sat down at the right hand of God.

20 They went forth, and preached everywhere, the Lord working with them, and confirming the word by the signs that followed. Amen.

The Resurrection

Mark 16:1-8: The resurrection is the most important truth of Christianity and the greatest hope of mankind. Jesus defeated death and, ultimately, all death will be destroyed. This is why the apostolic message was "they preached Jesus and the resurrection from the dead." There is no more powerful truth than the resurrection because the greatest yoke of bondage on mankind is fear. The greatest fear is the fear of death. When we believe in

our hearts in the resurrection, we will not live in fear of death. When this ultimate fear is broken, all others are easy to break.

He Appears to His Own

16:9-20: Like most Christians, the disciples knew the Lord's teachings about the resurrection, but they had trouble believing it when they needed to. It is much easier to believe a doctrine intellectually than it is to apply it to our lives and live it. We will not know how deeply we believe until we face circumstances that require our faith to walk in truth. This is why our faith must be tested.

The Lord's exhortation to "go into all the world" was not just geographical. We are to go into every field of occupation: government, education, business, the military, media and entertainment, sports, or wherever we are. We go as missionaries with the truth that can set others free—Jesus and the resurrection from the dead.

NOTES

The Gospel of Mark
Proper Names and Definitions

Abba: father

Abiathar: excellent father, father of the remnant, father of abundance

Abraham: father of a great multitude, exalted father

Alexander: one who assists men

Alphaeus: leader or chief

Andrew: a strong man, manly

Arimathea: a lion dead to the Lord

Barabbas: son of the father, son of shame, confusion

Bartholomew: son of Tolmai, a son that suspends the waters

Beelzebub: god of dung, god of flies

Bethany: the house of song, the house of affliction, place of unripe figs

Bethphage: house of my month, or of early figs

Bethsaida: house of fruits, or of food, or of snares, or of fishing

Caesar: title of Roman Emperors

Capernaum: the field of repentance, city of comfort, walled village

Christ: anointed

Cyrene: a wall, coldness, the floor

Dalmanutha: a bucket, a branch

David: well-beloved, dear

Decapolis: containing ten cities

Elijah: heifer, chariot, round, Yah is God

Ephphatha: be opened

Galilee: wheel, revolution, circle or circuit

Gennesaret: garden of the prince, of riches

Gentiles: the nations or pagan

Gerasenes: inhabitants of Gadara, meaning walls

Gethsemane: a very fat or plentiful vale

Golgotha: a heap of skulls, something skull-shaped

Herod: son of a hero, heroic

Hosanna: save I pray thee, keep, preserve

Isaac: laughter, he shall laugh, mockery

Isaiah: the salvation of the Lord

Iscariot: man of Kerioth, a man of murder, a hireling

Israel: who prevails with God, he shall be prince of God

Jacob: that supplants, undermines, heel-catcher

Jairus: my light, who diffuses light, he will awaken

James: that supplants, undermines, heel-catcher, he whom God protects

Jericho: his moon, his month, his sweet smell

Jerusalem: vision of peace, foundation of peace, restoring or teaching of peace

Jesus: savior, deliverer, Yahweh is salvation

John: the grace or mercy of the Lord

Jordan: the river of judgment, flowing downward, to bring down

Joseph: increase, addition, may God add

Judas: the praise of the Lord, confession

Legion: a great number

Levi: associated with him, joined

Magdalene: a person from Magdala, tower

Mary: bitterness, rebellion

Matthew: given, a reward, gift of Jehovah

Moses: taken out, drawn forth

Myrrh: bitter, symbolic of the graces of the Messiah

Nazareth: separated, crowned, sanctified, watchtower

Passover: to pass or to spring over, to spare

Peter: a rock or stone

Pharisees: set apart

Philip: warlike, a lover of horses

Philippi: warlike, a lover of horses

Pilate: armed with a dart, cap of freedom

Rabbi: my teacher

Rufus: red

Sadducees: followers of Sadoc, or Zadok, righteous

Salome: peaceable, perfect, he that rewards

Satan: contrary, adversary, enemy, accuser, deceiver

Sidon: hunting, fishing, venison

Simon: that hears, that obeys

Sin: bush, thorn

Tabitha: clear-sighted, a roe-deer

Thomas: a twin

Tyre: Tyrus, strength, rock, sharp

Zebedee: abundant, portion, gift of God